LEARNING TO FEEL

One Man's Path of Reconnecting to the
Heart of Emotions

Second Edition

KRIS GIRRELL

Copyright 2025

All rights reserved. No part of this book may be reproduced or utilized in any form or by any means, digital or mechanical, including photocopying, recording, or by any information and retrieval system, without permission in writing from the publisher.

For information, contact
MSI Press LLC
1760-F Airline Highway, #203
Hollister, CA 95023

Copyeditor: Lynne Curry

Cover design & book layout: Opeyemi Ikuborije

ISBN: 978-1-957354-73-6

Library of Congress Control Number: 2023900495

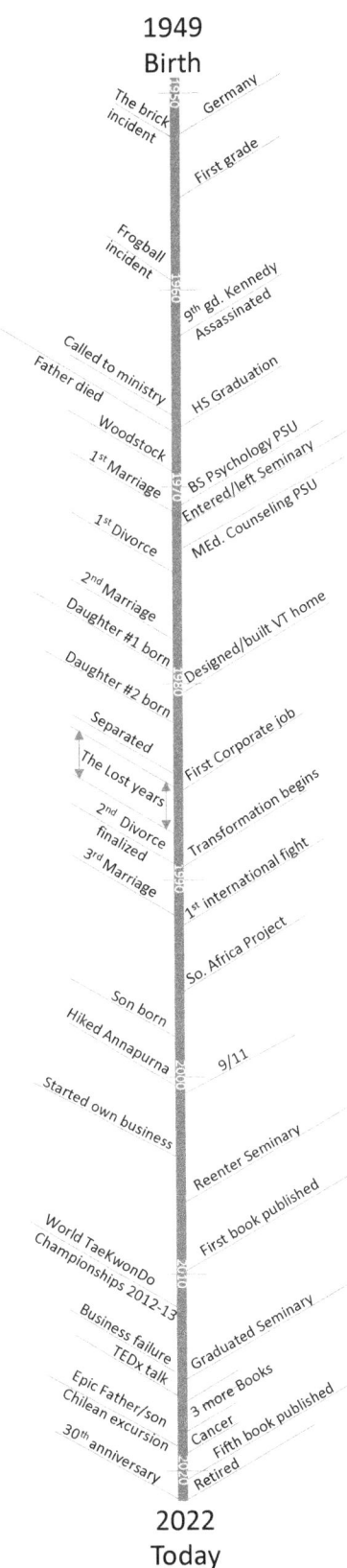

CONTENTS

Acknowledgements 1

Part One: Feeling From the Head Up

I Think I Feel. 5

Emotions Drive the Bus!. 9

We See the World as WE Are 17

Integrity and the Spartacus Moment. 23

Part Two: Developmental Pathways

When I Am a Hammer. 33

My Four-Legged Stool. 43

A Backdrop of Religion 55

Moral and Ethical Development. 61

To Love and Be Loved. 69

Part Three: Welcome to the Jungle

The Inner Journey of the "Hero's Quest" 79

Impasse, Failure, and Transformation. 85

Part Four: A Rainbow of Emotions

Naming Emotions 97

A Periodic Table of Human Emotions 105

Experiencing Emotions 111

Learning Compassion 117

Part Five: Finding Emotions and Emotional Intelligence

The Red Thread 125

A model for presence 131

Meditation and Presence 135

Becoming Emotionally Intelligent 139

Epilogue to the Second Edition 151

Works Cited 153

Songs 157

Learning to feel will definitely make you feel better:

- *feel joy better.*
- *feel pain better.*
- *feel sadness better.*
- *and feel a lot more love.*
  - *You just feel better!*

LEARNING TO FEEL

Acknowledgements

I have been blessed to be surrounded by great colleagues and friends, and in writing this book, that has been invaluable. First and foremost, I must thank Sarah, my wife, for her insistence that I do the deep work of introspection and discovery. She is both my biggest supporter and my driving force.

Additionally, throughout this book I have mentioned several other close friends who have been part of this process:

> Andy Chaleff, an accomplished leadership and emotional intelligence coach. In my opinion, Andy is an advanced master and as such has taught me so much. It was through Andy's guidance that I not only started this project but experimented with the vulnerability of weaving in my own personal history and experiences.

> Amy Bladen Shatto, a brilliant psychologist, coach and business consultant with deep expertise in leadership development. Amy has been my peer and colleague for many years, and we have enjoyed many projects and adventures together. Though I have often been her mentor and coach, in this project, we reversed the roles, and she has been my coach on the experience of writing personal material.

> Stacy Feiner, another psychologist friend who has been a colleague for over 20 years. Stacy and I have partnered on writing the standards and practices for the coaching industry and has been in and out of my life over these past many years. But since the start of the pandemic, we have grown even closer as friends and colleagues.

Of course, there are others, too many to list, who have been not only a part of my life and development but who have participated in reading sections and versions of this text.

To all of you, I love you. You are so much a part of me, and I am eternally indebted to you for all you have given.

Part One:
Feeling From the Head Up

LEARNING TO FEEL

1

I Think I Feel

"I still don't think you've done the deep work on yourself," Sarah told me.

"What do you mean? I have gone to therapy and done tons of work to discover the source of it," I defended.

"But you haven't uncovered the real issue, in my opinion," she replied. "What were you feeling that caused you to do that?"

Sarah has been my marriage partner and partner in life over the last thirty plus years and, at the same time, the thorn in my side who won't permit me to ignore or step over issues. We were talking about a time in our marriage quite some time ago when I allowed myself to fall into a sexually flirtatious email exchange with an old flame. It was a painful time that was almost the undoing of our marriage. While I have journaled on it and gone to therapy on it, all in the effort to discover what in me would allow or cause such an action, her claim that there is still more to uncover is persistent and lands on me as hauntingly true.

Don't get me wrong. I have done "The Work," going deep into my unconscious to unearth the beliefs and self-concepts that drive my every action. And what, in particular, Sarah has been quick to point out is that I have never felt as if I'm enough. There has always been something inside me that continues to seek validation outside myself or my marriage.

I know that I am not alone in this regard!

It is an age-old challenge that many of us face, and it all begins when we were little tykes. Psychologists tell us that we learn 90% of our vocabulary before the age of five. All of our polysyllabic, fancy words we use in adulthood represent less than 10% of our full working vocabulary. And since the bulk of those words we were learning as little ones described objects and situations in the world around us, 90% of the concepts we have about the world were learned at that same time. The issue is that when we were learning our words, everything around us was bigger, faster, stronger, and smarter than we were and that, therefore, we were not (big, fast, strong, or smart).

Adults and the world around us taught us that we were just little and not very powerful. That's why when we learn our first power words *no* and *mine* (usually around two years old), we exercise them as often as we can just to try and have some control over our world. Of course, we then find out that our *no* is not as powerful as mom's or dad's and that adds to the belief that we are not enough. Not good enough, not fast enough, not powerful enough, not smart enough. Not enough. And in that moment, we adopted one of two beliefs that drive our behaviors for a good portion of the rest of our lives:

- We overachieve: "Oh, yeah, I'll show you that I am something! Watch this."
- We underachieve: "Oh, (sigh), I guess I really am just nothing but a squirt."

You will certainly recognize one of those scripts as yours. For me, it was the former. For the bulk of my adult years I have been pushing myself to prove that I really am enough. But if the underpinning of that drive is the real belief that I am *not* enough, then nothing I accomplish will ever convince me of anything else. That is the inner work Sarah was referring to. It is not sufficient to discover the source of those beliefs—family of origin, daycare, teachers, or other adults and older siblings—one must be able to uproot them at the source and eradicate the beliefs altogether, supplanting them with new and more functional beliefs. Perhaps equally as important as that uprooting process is the fact that for all those years where I was operating from a place of not enough, I was also actively suppressing my true feelings. After all, if I am not enough, then my feelings would not be enough, or appropriate, or worthwhile as well.

It may seem strange for a person whose career was built on psychology, theology, and emotional intelligence to admit that he was not fully aware of how feelings were *experienced*, but that truth has been part and parcel of my development over the last two decades or so. It is one thing to be able to rattle off a bunch of emotion names and even to be able to define each as distinct from the other, but it is quite another thing to have the understanding of those emotions by virtue of having felt and experienced them.

In a 2016 TEDx talk I delivered,[1] I told the audience that same message: that I had studied emotions and taught emotional intelligence for a good chunk of my career but, with the exception of perhaps the purer feelings of love, anger, and joy, it was more or less a cognitive understanding that I had. In that talk, I told the audience about how, by virtue of dealing with deep loss and sadness, I had been opened up to the experience of many more emotions.

There is also an additional complicating factor that suppressed my emotional development—that is the simple fact that I am a man and grew up in a time when boys and men were taught not to feel. Through sports, I learned to deny my feelings. Pain, I was told, was weakness leaving the body. Anger was not useful because it blinded you from seeing what needed to be done. As a wrestler, I was taught that anger would cloud my thinking and result in defeat. And as a football player, my coach would often say of any minor injury (like a dislocated finger or a cut), "Spit on it and rub it in the dirt. You'll get over it." Yes, that is an actual quote!

In his seminal book, *I Don't Want to Talk About It*, therapist Terrence Real refers to the ritual wounding of boys as one of the foundations of this socialization to bury our emotions.

> Boys don't need to be turned into males. They are males. Boys don't need to develop their masculinity. They are masculine, no less than girls are feminine. Once we understand that "masculine identity" is not about an internal structure but rather a socially accepted definition of what it means to be male, then the processes by which we impose those definitions on boys sharpens into clarity. [This] passage from boyhood to manhood is about ritual wounding. It is about giving up those parts of the self that do not fit within the confines of the role. It is about pain and the withstanding of pain… These emotional amputations can be effected through active or passive injury, in transactions severe or seemingly mild.[2]

As boys growing up in the 1950s, we were all taught that "big boys don't cry." Feelings were scoffed at as not objective or real information. Even as an adult, I had a friend who, when asked if he felt things, would always quip, "I feel; I feel with my hands!" Though that was always said in jest, that view was something most other men could relate to and chuckled about. Oh, there were times as a kid when I quietly cried myself to sleep so as not to let my brother hear me, but the messaging was clear and ubiquitous: Feelings just got in the way. It didn't help much to be told that I was gifted with an intellect, so as a result, I began to process everything through my thinking. I would even say such things as "I think I feel" rather than simply going to the feeling.

---

1. Kris Girrell, "How We've Been Misled by Emotional Intelligence, " TED video, 14:34. https://www.youtube.com/watch?v=6l8yPt8S2gE.

2. Terrence Real, *I Don't Want to Talk About It* (New York: Scribner, 1997), 132-133.

There were many times as a young adult when I found myself saying that I didn't know how I should feel or how to feel it. There were (and still are) complex situations wherein a number of emotional responses well up. And this was true even into my mid-years, at 50, when I had traveled to Kathmandu and was sitting near the banks of the sacred Bagmati River. On the far side of the river there were three funeral pyres. A father was having his head shaved as a mark of his mourning for the child who had died, whose pyre burned nearby. Just above them were two temples, one of which was having a very festive wedding ceremony. On my side of the river there were children and older women selling garnet necklaces and silver jewelry. And beside them there were the sadhu, yogis who live on goat's milk alone and who could contort their thin but aged bodies in the most unusual ways—asking if you want to take their picture—for a few rupees, of course. At any moment one could feel sad, joyful, pitiful, curious, compassionate, and fascinated—and often all of those landed at the same time. Trying to process that as a combined set of feelings was confusing, to say the least, and is complicated by the socialization we males had undergone.

It is possible to go through life with a working tool kit of just a handful of basic emotions—happiness, anger, sadness, and a few others—but it is quite limiting to have to force fit all experiences into those big buckets of general emotions. And the result of having a limited set of emotional labels is that it further impacts the number of limiting self-beliefs we end up with. So, these two vectors—learning that we are not enough and learning that our emotions are either in the way or limited in their capacity to describe and process the world and our experience of it—collide in a way that becomes an impediment at the very least and debilitating in the worst-case scenario.

It is that mashup of half-baked skills, forgotten memories, strange and unusual experiences, and the interpretations they all left me with that resulted in my being rather ill-equipped to answer Sarah's challenge of figuring it all out. It was a challenge I finally needed to accept.

Questions to ponder:

1. When do you remember having strong feelings that just didn't fit the words you had to label them?

2. How has your gender effected your ability to experience your emotions?

3. What have been the consequences you have experienced when feeling something deeply?

2

Emotions Drive the Bus!

Sarah catches me over the dinner table with what occurs to me as a random—out of the blue—question, but which for her is a continuation of her inquiry:

"How did it feel when your first wife broke up with you?"

"Honestly, I don't remember how I was feeling. I guess I felt numb."

"Well, you must have had a conversation or something when she made that announcement. Can't you remember any of it?"

"I remember feeling sad and I remember one day riding the train into work and—it was a rainy day—and the rain rolling down the window seemed to map onto the reflection of my face as I stared out. But really, that's all I can recall."

"I find it hard to believe that you didn't at least talk about it."

I would be willing to wager that while most of us know we have feelings, being able to access those feeling is somehow altogether different and more challenging. When we were children, feelings came over us and we didn't know why they were happening—just that they were happening. And as children, we experienced them, and then they were gone and done with. I am quite fond of Dr. Brené Brown, who has spent her career studying emotions and, in particular, those of guilt, shame, and vulnerability. During an interview she had about her latest book *Atlas of the Heart*,³ she had this observation about emotions in general. "Let me be clear: Emotion is at the wheel. Thinking and acting are not in the front seat, riding shotgun. They are hogtied in the trunk. Emotion drives. We are emotional beings." If emotions are the lead drivers, then what should we learn about them and how do we go about this task?

Maybe a better question is what good are emotions and why are we humans "blessed" with them or the ability to "feel" in the first place? The answer to that question is a tad more complex than the scope of this discussion allows, but the short answer seems to be that emotions were part of the survival system we developed through evolution. In essence, the function of emotions is to drive our actions—they tell us what to do. Emotions want to drive quick responses as survival techniques, but often our initial emotional reaction (which, as we will see, is filtered through our beliefs and self-concepts) may not be as optimal or accurate as we may wish. For example, you leave a message for a friend, and your friend does not return the call. Your initial reaction may be hurt, frustration, or anger and may result in your snapping when your friend does call you back, when in actuality your friend could have had some serious challenge and just couldn't get back to you immediately. You had an emotional reaction, but it was clouded by your thought, your self-concepts, and your previous experiences of your friend.

Thus, since that function is not just to feel but to act, listening to our emotions and learning to skillfully experience them so that we have a clearer sense of what action we should take are much different than just feeling them. This book, *Learning to Feel*, is really about how to experience our emotions on a clearer and deeper level such that we begin moving in a more emotionally connected direction.

> **But the bigger, overarching purpose of this book focuses on one goal—enabling readers to find some tools to tap into their own feelings and understand the messages and power of their own emotions. To accomplish that objective, my fervent hope is that readers will draw lessons from understanding the issues that have blocked my emotions and made them less accessible to me.**

In order to do that we need to look into how our emotions are made (from whence they come) and then be clear enough with our own personal developmental path that we can trust that the emotions are unfiltered and giving us clearer messages. I am not going to go into the neuroscience of how emotions occur and how the brain and central nervous system produce them. For an in-depth but clearly articulated answer, I would refer you to Lisa Feldman Barrett's book, *How Emotions are Made: The Secret Life of the Brain*.⁴ What Barrett and her colleagues in the field of brain research have found is that emotions are

---

3. Brené Brown, *Atlas of the Heart: Mapping Meaningful Connection and the Language of Human Experience* (New York: Penguin Random House, 2021).

4. Lisa Feldman Barrett, *How Emotions are Made: The Secret Life of the Brain* (New York: Houghton Mifflin, 2017).

manufactured by the brain. What goes into that process comes from a variety of sources ranging from genetics to bodily sensations, experiences, social learning, and the continual deep functioning of the brain's operating system.

As a broad generalization, psychology has held that there are regions of the brain that are responsible for various functions. Each function—hearing, seeing, smelling, along with planning, motivation, memory, and so on— was associated with a given region of the brain that then was processed by what was referred to as the limbic brain and amygdala. However, most of that physical mapping of the brain was conducted on brain injuries in live patients (we really couldn't learn much from a corpse). So, when a patient would come in with an injury to the side of the head and be unable to speak, the obvious deduction was that the area controlling speech must be in the region that was injured.

But now that scientists and researchers can monitor activities of the brain using live imaging technology, these live scans show not only that all parts of the brain are actively engaged in all aspects of sensation and perception, the entire brain is also active in creating emotional responses as well. What research is uncovering is that there is continual activity going on in the brain at all times. This immense volume of activity, called the intrinsic brain activity or the intrinsic network, is a continual cascade of neuron firings on a massive scale. Much of that activity is just keeping us alive by causing the heart to beat and our lungs, diaphragm, and upper body to keep breathing. But it is also the source of our daydreaming, imagination, reverie, and mental wandering off on tangents. And our emotions.

To oversimplify this part of the discussion, essentially the ongoing, intrinsic system is continually taking new information received through bodily sensations and external stimuli, comparing that with the billions of stored memories, experiences, and sensations and then "predicting" or projecting that on the next moment and out into the future. If the compared database contains scary memories, the projection includes the possibility of fear. If the associated information was pleasurable, our brain will predict goodness or happiness. However, Barrett writes, "Emotions are not reactions to the world. You are not a passive receiver of sensory input but an active constructor of your emotions. From sensory input and past experience, your brain constructs meaning and prescribes action." She continues a few pages later, "Through prediction, your brain constructs the world you experience. It combines bits and pieces of your past and estimates how likely each bit applies in your current situation."[5]

But let's get back to the discussion of why we have emotions in the first place. How this all evolved is the source of another great debate. Evolutionists contend that our emotions evolved as a function of our need for survival. Back in prehistory when we upright

---

5. Barrett, *How Emotions Are Made*, 59.

hominids coexisted with predators that could easily be our undoing by consuming one of us for lunch, we needed to know how and when to fight, flee, feed, or freeze on the spot. These, among other sensations associated with survival, became our core emotions and then the brain went to work on refinements on those basic feelings.

Cognitive theorists contend that the evolution of emotions derive more from the ability of the brain to think of itself. That introspection and self-perception resulted in further evaluations which moved us into the realm of emotions and emotional development. But both of these theories smack of emotions being the source; that is, emotions spontaneously evolved and happen as a result of our evolution and worldly situations—somewhat contrary to the findings of current brain research. Whether our emotions come from one of these roots or are simply the evolved functions of an active processing system held somewhere between our ears, we have come equipped with these emotive gifts. Evolution has hardwired our brains to become accurate and efficient prediction machines.

That's nice, but it is only one part of the story. Our brains are continually monitoring somatic data of both gross bodily movements and internal organs and systems. Despite our powers of prediction, those predictions are continually integrated with information the body is generating. If and when all of these line up, the prediction stands. But that is the rare occasion. More likely what occurs are a series of prediction errors immediately followed by corrective actions, predictions, and further corrections.

Take, for example, walking on a moving sidewalk in the airport. Your body is moving at the rate of speed of the sidewalk plus your walking rate of speed. You have the somatic perception of going faster than those people walking on the floor next to you and of your conveyor belt. So cognitively, you are aware of the fact that there will be a rate change and an adjustment to your pace when the moving sidewalk comes to an end. But it's a prediction (if your experience is anything like mine) that is usually inaccurate: The surprise of your bodily adjustments to that rate change sent back to your brain causes you to have to adjust more than you had predicted. The consequences of making slight (and sometimes much larger) prediction errors feed back into the brain's self-awareness function as a new set of beliefs or as confirmation of your inferiority (I'm not ____ enough).

So what? What are the implications of being emotional creatures? All of these predictions, sensations, corrections, and re-predictions continually loop through the intrinsic system as a backdrop to your conscious life, conscious predictions, and the emotions that those produce. Despite this new research, most of the field of psychology and sociology still cling to a mechanical model of brain functioning which includes emotions as more spontaneously generated by the limbic brain. So, when we begin a discussion of emotions, self-concepts, limiting self-beliefs, and so on, we must take caution in assuming what our feelings mean before we are able to reverse-engineer them in our attempt to change or alter the substrate concepts we hold onto in our minds.

I was trained originally in behavioral psychology, and the bulk of my work as a consultant has been in creating and interpreting behavioral assessments and behavioral/competency models for corporate clients. What that translates into is that most of my professional work has been looking at, inspecting, and interpreting only the parts of the person that shows up. But behaviors are like the tip of an iceberg, and the parts we don't see, like the 90% of the iceberg that is beneath the surface of the water, is a little harder to discern. That was fine for me because working with executives and corporate types, I didn't have to go into the world of "fluffy" emotions and personality traits. Part of my training also included the use of those personality assessments, and I feel that I have a great deal of mastery in their use and interpretation. Irrespective of that, I still would port that back to how they made a person behave. So, I am neither avoiding the topics of emotions and personality nor am I afraid of their murky meanings. It's just that I related more to the behaviors and found reinforcement for that interpretation in my clients.

The truth of the matter is that despite new breakthroughs in brain research, we know very little about how the brain does its work of creating emotions—only that it does. Delving into emotions is science-based guess-work at the best. My intellectual snobbery perhaps held some disdain for going deeper on my own quest to understand them in the way I am now learning how to understand them and to extrapolate those experiences into self-concepts and referential foundations for future interpretations.

This book is an effort not only to inspect the way in which we go about finding and uprooting our limiting self-beliefs, but it is also an investigation into how doing so alters our awareness of emotions, our emotional states, and our emotional intelligence. The bottom line is learning how to take all that into account in a way that reports in on how I learned and am learning how to feel. Amy Bladen-Shatto is an industrial-organizational psychologist whom I have been mentoring in the art of coaching for several years. Now it is her turn at the wheel as *my* coach. I was stuck on how to write about myself and yet not have it be too strangely autobiographical in nature.

> Me: I am having a difficult time getting started with this project.
>
> Coach: Have you ever tried free writing?
>
> Me: Yes, in fact several times quite successfully, I might add.
>
> Coach: Might I suggest that you start writing without knowing what your plan or outline is and see what comes out?
>
> Me: I'm not sure what you mean.
>
> Coach: Take one of these conversations from the past that you have difficulty recalling, and just start writing out what you might imagine was the conversation. Perhaps that process will jog some other memories that then resurrect others.

> Me: Hmm, well I have never written a book or essay that way, but I'm willing to give it a go and see what turns up.

As I write this, I am aware that I am the laboratory in which much of what I believe and feel can be and will be inspected and analyzed. However, my challenge to you will be to apply these little expeditions into the realm of recalled feelings for yourself through a set of questions at the end of each section. I do not assume my experience to be yours, yet I also know that 99.9% of our DNA is identical, so we most likely have many experiences and emotions in common. Additionally, because of my profession, I have the luxury of having worked with thousands of others and will at times be bringing those conversations and their experiences around emotions and emotional intelligence into the narrative. Just as a sidenote, with the exception of myself and my wife, whom you have already met by name, I will change elements of the conversations and descriptions of those other people to protect their anonymity. But, trust me, they are all very real people.

As I have said, psychology teaches us that our emotions are the result of our thoughts that are derived from and based in our beliefs about ourselves and the world in which we live. Throughout, the book will be investigating how emotions are formed and what their internal message is. We will pull apart what emotional intelligence entails and look into how to develop a stronger and more functional emotional intellect. And we will look at how we can access our full emotional experience, learning what it can provide and how it benefits us.

One last thought on why we should learn about emotions: My friend Dr. Stacy Feiner calls emotions our superpower.[6] It's not just our emotions that are the superpower—it's the ability to recognize them, know them, respond appropriately to them and to be able to do the same with others. That is the simplest definition of emotional intelligence, and I will dedicate an entire chapter to EI later in the book.

But Stacy's point is about more than just having emotional intelligence. It's all about becoming emotionally mature. She says it is a basic knowing—an understanding of oneself, a visceral knowing. The trick to this knowing, however, is that we must learn how to trust our core emotions. I use the term "core" emotions to distinguish them from those emotions we have as a result of our thoughts and worries. Most of us spend way more time in the past (agonizing over what we could have, should have, and would have done) or fretting over the future (anxious about what might happen and the wondering about all the what-ifs).

---

6. Dr. Stacy Feiner, "You Are My Why—The Deliberate Mind & the Unconscious Mind," August 11, 2022, LinkedIn, https://www.linkedin.com/in/stacyfeiner/recent-activity/posts/.

Those are the thoughts, as Feldman describes them, that produce the bulk of what we experience as emotions. But there are also emotions that stem from our physical being. We know that our medulla (the inner part of our brain stem that controls all autonomic systems) is perpetually monitoring what is going on in our body. It perceives, for example, that when we are in the embrace of our lover, we are safe and loved, and as a result, we relax and feel calm. Conversely, when we put on our work attire, we prepare ourselves to handle the onslaught of things that work throws at us, and the body is slightly more tensed. That happens irrespective of the past/future machinations of our cortical brain.

When we get to a point of emotional maturity, we can trust our inner emotional gyroscope to guide our actions in an appropriate direction—one that serves our soul, our values, and our life goals. Digging in the fertile soil of our past, we may be able to remove what clogs the system (like negative self-talk, limiting beliefs, guilt, shame, and the rest of those learned but buried thoughts), shift our ways of being, and learn to feel in a clean, clear and unencumbered way. You may not feel the need to write a book—that's just my way of doing the work. But the questions I provide at the end of each chapter may help you in your quest.

Questions to ponder:

1. Would you consider yourself to be emotionally mature or emotionally intelligent?

2. Of the emotions you are most familiar with, which would say you have fully experienced and which would you consider that you only "know about"?

3. Where do you experience your emotions physically—where in your body do you feel?

LEARNING TO FEEL

3

We See the World as WE Are

Let me start this with a little true story:

> When I was a child, my family lived in Germany on a military base. We kids played outside on the stoop and sidewalks since there were not any playgrounds to speak of. On one particular day I was on the landing outside the entrance playing with a truck or some cool toy. The others were scattered around the sidewalk three or four steps down from the landing. When asked if I would share my toy with the others, I refused and was very possessive about it. This set the other children off and they started teasing and mocking me for being "stingy."
>
> The more they taunted me the angrier I got until I hit some sort of breaking point. I was as enraged as a four-year-old boy could be. Standing up, I noticed one of the bricks—a half brick, actually—along the side of the steps that was loose. In my anger, I picked it up and threw it at the other kids and it struck one of the boys on the side of the head. His face and head were a bloody mess in a matter of seconds and I got frightened. I ran into the apartment and hid under the kitchen table.

This vision was something I carried with me for decades, along with the lesson that I was a mean and hurtful person who could do damage. But in my late thirties, I was attending a transformational training that challenged us to unearth and check into our long-held self-concepts. In the process, that memory popped up. So I decided to call my sister who, at two years my elder, was my constant companion and protector when we were kids. Though she remembered the time I hid under the table crying, she did not recall the brick incident. She recommended I call our mother. Mom's answer was clear and shocking. "Living in the barracks," she said, "we mothers were always in contact with each other. If *anything* like that had happened, I would have known about it immediately. That never happened."

Wait. What? This event that was so clearly remembered, so vivid a memory in my mind, never happened? Then what really (must have) happened was that a little boy (who, by the way, had neither the strength or the physical acumen to throw a brick and actually hit someone with it) was so angry that he made up a scene he only *wished* could be. It became a memory as strong as any real experience I had growing up. Not only that, but it had become the foundation of a belief that I was mean, evil, and hurtful, and could do damage to others. As I grew into being a large man, this memory and belief was extrapolated to my strength and physical abilities. I had to be careful, because I could easily hurt someone!

But learning that it never happened was profound—I might even call it earthshaking. I suddenly was released from the belief in my latent violent tendencies. I was lifted out of the self-imposed darkness in which I had been operating for most of my life. Not only was I freed, I became skeptical of my deepest held beliefs about myself. How, then, do I know what is real and what is interpreted or even made up? This epistemological quandary has both haunted and served me ever since.

How do we know what we know? The great philosopher René Descartes (the "I think therefore I am" guy) found that same thing to be true himself. He realized the power of the mind to make reality out of fantasy and became skeptical of any of his own, untested thoughts.

> "All that up to the present time I have accepted as most true and certain I have learned either from the senses or through the senses; but it is sometimes proved to me that these senses are deceptive, and it is wiser not to trust entirely to anything by which we have once been deceived . . . I suppose, then, that all the things that I see are false; I persuade myself that nothing has ever existed of all that my fallacious memory represents to me. I consider that I possess no senses; I imagine that body, figure, extension, movement and place are but the fictions of my mind. What, then, can be esteemed as true? Perhaps nothing at all, unless that there is nothing in the world that is certain."[7]

Put another way, in a maxim attributed to Anaïs Nin but which may date all the way back to the *Talmud*, "We don't see the world as it is, but as we are." So the question becomes, how do we know what is reality and what is truth—or at least what is our truth? Like Descartes, I know my mind has the ability to make sense out of what it gets as input, but

---

7. René Descartes, "Meditations on First Philosophy," *Internet Encyclopedia of Philosophy* (1996). This file is of the 1911 edition of *The Philosophical Works of Descartes* (Cambridge University Press), translated by Elizabeth S. Haldane.

I am skeptical of its deductive reasoning. Of course, we must agree that there are simple things that are part of objective reality we would all agree upon. That is a chair and this is a table. I am writing a book or what I presume will become a book, and an outside observer watching me would probably conclude the same. So, I am not skeptical of all of my thoughts, just my interpretations, the interpretive thoughts that have to do with who I am and what I believe about myself and the world of my creation.

Every event in our lives basically consists of three elements. There is the experience itself—what actually, factually happened. Then there is what I would call the experience of the experience. In other words, let's say a tree falls in the forest while I am hiking one day. The experience is that a tree fell down. But my experience of the experience of that tree falling is surprise (or perhaps fear if it happened to fall very close to me). The third element is what we might call the interpretation of the experience. That is what our mind does to make sense of the experience. I could perhaps take the interpretation that I am blessed and have a guardian angel watching out for me such that I was unscathed by the falling tree. Another interpretation could be that things like that are always happening to me and that I am a magnet for danger. And, of course there are probably a dozen more interpretations we could take of that one situation.

Over time these experiences and interpretations become the filter through which everything else is then perceived. The mind will make interpretations and then seeks confirmations of those interpretations in future events. By the time we have become adults, there have been billions of billions of such experiences and interpretations stored in our minds. Then, everything else will be measured and compared to that data base. Everything that we perceive comes in through that filter and everything we say goes out through that filter. You and I could literally have the same experience together and come away with two completely different interpretations or understandings of that event. We could both witness the same traffic accident and touch the same bent fender, and yet we will file two different traffic reports.

What Descartes was referring to in his skepticism was not the perceived experience nor his experience of the experience. It was his *interpretation*, the story his mind made up about the experience, that he did not trust. And the same is true for me and you. Our self-concepts are constructed not of the experiences of our lives but rather from the stories we construct from our interpretations of those events and experiences.

Sarah and I can have a discussion one evening about what we are going to be doing the next day and so I will get up and start working. Shortly thereafter, Sarah will come into the room and ask what I am doing. I will most likely say something like "This is what we talked about doing last night." "No we didn't," she'll retort. "We discussed doing . . . (something I had not "heard")." How, then could the two of us be in the same conversation and have come away with two different interpretations?

And that is, as I said, the overarching "why" behind this book—to learn why I am who I am, or who I have become—and in the process also discover why I do what I do. In doing so, my desire is also to help you to discover some of the same. "Owning our story can be hard but not nearly as difficult as spending our lives running from it," says social science researcher, Dr. Brené Brown. "Only when we are brave enough to explore the darkness will we discover the infinite power of our light."[8]

This is no simple task! For most of us, we cannot really tell the difference between the events of our lives and the interpretations we made of them. I have a friend who would always preface her opinions with the phrase, "Well, the fact is . . ." I would point out that it was not fact but was instead her perception of what happened and would try to help her separate her beliefs and opinions from the observable events. While she was unbelievably intelligent, it took years of doing that for her to understand that her perceptions often were not held by others—even other very smart people. Mostly this was because, as an extremely intelligent person, she had thought through all of the possibilities she was aware of and had arrived at her "obvious" conclusion. Her underlying belief was that if others did not see these things as "fact," then they must not be very smart!

Eventually she would change her preface to "It's my opinion that the facts of the situation are," but there was still that belief that if others didn't share that view, they were of lesser intellect. After many years of practice, she now asks others what they have observed and begins by challenging her own interpretation with their new information. In doing so, she has opened her eyes and now can see how each of us can see the same event and have different interpretation of that event. Furthermore, she sees that diversity as a beautiful element of the human experience.

Sometimes it takes a powerful event to shake us out of this strongly held belief, and sometimes it is a slow, unfolding process. But in order to do the work of discerning the whys and the wherefores of our underlying beliefs and meaning-making structures, we must get to that realization that we have, in "fact," interpreted the event. And it is the interpretation that lives on inside of us (not the event). The event occurred and passed long ago, but the memory and interpretative story about that event is what continues.

So to return to the Cartesian skepticism, what we are challenged to do in learning how to feel (as in learning how to have good, effective, and useful feelings that would guide us in the best direction) is this ability to separate events from our interpretations and hold those interpretations with some degree of distrust.

You may never really know the full factual truth about life events and may come to the realization that truth and fact are only personal interpretations, but at least we can

---

8. Brené Brown, *Daring Greatly: How the Courage to Be Vulnerable Transforms the Way We Live, Love, Parent, and Lead* (New York: Penguin Random House, 2015).

become more aware of the differences and distinctions. From that place we can begin to understand what our emotions are telling us and whether that is something on which we should act or not.

> **Questions to ponder**
>
> 1. How confident are you about your perception of "reality?" What causes you to question reality or at least your perception of it?
>
> 2. How might you become more conscious of the thoughts that are at the source of your emotions and emotional states?
>
> 3. How have you begun "owning your interpretations," and if you have not yet taken that on, what might get you started on that path?

4

Integrity and the Spartacus Moment

David Deida and Ken Wilber are great friends. Deida, an author and trainer in the realm of intimacy and relationships, once wrote an essay about his friend, Ken Wilber, perhaps the foremost philosopher of our time. The essay entitled "Ken Wilber is a Fraud"[9] claimed that Wilber's gift to humanity was that he lived at the cutting edge of human experience. His role in life was to stick his face in the cosmos and venture into new and original patterns of thought. Thus, his job, Deida claims, is to think the thoughts that have not yet been "thunk" [sic]. And it demands a kind of bold and brutal honesty that Wilber violated because of his gentle compassionate nature. When Ken made it worse by stepping out of his "role" to be an author and, what he calls, "a pundit," to report on his thoughts and thought process, that, says his buddy, moved him into the realm of the fraudulent.

Deida does this with complete love and admiration for his friend, who, in turn, thanked him for the tongue-in-cheek critique. But the bottom line is that the philosopher must always and at all times *be* a philosopher—not the reporter, not the compassionate lover, and not even a friend. There must be that brutal honesty to his work that Wilbur, in Deida's experience, no longer was demonstrating when he was writing or teaching.

I am no Ken Wilber nor even qualified to breathe the same rarified air he breathes. I am nowhere as intelligent or as mentally disciplined. But there is an analogy to what I do as a self-described psychologist. I, too, am a fraud in that my job requires understanding

---

9. While I was not able to find the original essay on David Deida's website, the full essay is available here: "Ken Wilbur Is a Fraud," https://sckool.org/essays--editors-note.html.

emotions—what they are, from whence they come, what they mean to us, and guide us. And for the most part, I conceptually "understand" and can teach that (and have on many occasions). But the fraudulent part is that I am not so certain that I have actually lived and experienced the fullness of my emotions. In fact, I am fairly certain that my "knowledge of" emotions is not the same as the "experience of" those emotions. In other words, to further complicate the process of "knowing" discussed in the last chapter, I have the additional problem of knowing but not understanding—and understanding is actually part of my job, as a psychologist.

To be true to form, my job description should include understanding emotions from an experiential perspective. But the problem of doing so is twofold. First of all, we all face the dilemma and difficulty of being present to our experience–or what I might call the experience of the experience. The instant that we are having an experience– emotional or physical—our mind kicks into high gear to try to understand, classify, and label it. That thought about the experience is no longer the experience—it is a story about or a report on the experience. Like Ken Wilber reporting back from the cosmos, it is no longer being in the experience of pure and original thought or emotion. The report and the label of the emotional experience is not the emotion and is not even of the same realm.

The second issue is having the emotional experience in the first place. Religious scholar and author, Joseph Campbell once said that the best way to ensure that you will not have a true experience is to have studied it beforehand. With a career in psychology and having been way overeducated in that field, I am almost guaranteed not to have a pure experience of emotions. Those feelings, having been studied, sliced and diced beforehand, will almost invariably be experienced through the filter of what I had learned they should be.

To make matters worse, we all have our emotional experiences shaped by our history of other events, experiences, socialization, education, family of origin, religion, and . . . the list goes on quite extensively. The question then becomes: What are our true feelings? And right on the heels of that: How do we begin the process of rediscovering emotions?

Since *Learning to Feel* is a combination of personal exploration and scholarly research into the experience and use of emotions and emotional intelligence, we will need to look at what gets in the way of our pure emotive experience and what we can do to dissolve or at least lower the barriers between us and the full experience of emotions so that we might be able, once again, to live with them, learn from them, and use them as evolution has deigned we should.

My friend and transformational trainer Chris Hawker starts one of his sessions drawing a cute face of a smiling child (actually just a circle with two eye dots and a big smile). He says we all start life out with only two fears: the fear of falling and the fear of loud noises. And for the most part, we are happy just to be—to be alive and to be in the experience of the experience of living. But then, Hawker says, as he draws a black line through the happy face, someone hurts us, tells us "no!" or that we can't do that. Then we have a negative experience (another slash across the happy face), and another and another. Each time we have been hurt, thwarted, told no, repressed or otherwise had that innocence crushed, another line goes on the drawing until there are so many that you can't see the smiling happy child's face at all! And that is where we find ourselves as adults. It is not a conscious effort to delude others or to be a fraud by no longer feeling fully. It is a natural reaction to the many things that have suppressed our experiencing those feelings.

I no longer want to be a fraud (I never did *want* it). And I am making the assumption that you do not want to be fraudulent either. So it is my hope that this process of exploring, discovering, and relearning the whats and how-tos of emotions, and emotional intelligence will be a guide for the many others who have found it difficult or challenging to experience and use their emotions. Through a combination of deconstructing my personal experiences and those of others, woven together with the latest brain science and classic studies in the science of emotion, I want to once again feel those pure emotions (I need not feel all of them—just the ones that appropriately come up) and regain some degree of authenticity in the process.

The bottom line is one of getting closer to a level of emotional intelligence that is based in a clear and accurate self-awareness. Both being aware of the difference between the experience and the interpretation of that experience, and being aware of how much I do or do not "know" my true depth of feelings are essential to being fully self-aware. When pursuing emotional intelligence, most of us focus our attention on trying to understand what another person is feeling. But in order to do that with any degree of accuracy, we first must be conscious of our own feeling state and how it may be coloring our perceptions of others.

I imagine that many men, who have been programmed to feel only feelings of anger and numbness, who may want to shake off those bonds and begin rediscovering what full access to their emotions can be, will find this valuable as well. But it is not just meant for men. Emotions are the realm of all humans—and, for that matter, of all mammals. We have all read stories of the dogs who after the passing of their human make the nightly trek to the graveyard to sleep next their deceased friend. And I have personally witnessed the frantic chipping of a chipmunk whose buddy had fallen into my swimming pool. It was inconsolably running back and forth as its friend paddled in the water to keep its head above the surface until it was rescued. I am fairly certain that the chipmunk was not thinking about what the future would be like without its friend or remembering all the good times they had had together. It was simply, purely distressed about its friend and about the experience of not being able to do anything to help.

My friends have a service dog who instinctively knows when one of them is feeling stress or has gotten hurt and knows how to sit by them and comfort them. He is, at the time of this writing, still somewhat of a puppy, and as such loves to play. But the moment he senses anyone being hurt or in distress, he stops playing and immediately moves into service. His sensitivity and awareness supersede any thoughts about playing. There is no fraudulent aspect of that dog. He is on purpose and ready to be emotionally aware at all times.

We all have emotions and they serve us well. And while the dogs and the chipmunks can't read or write, I suppose they would have a lot to teach us about experiencing pure emotions. Perhaps, we were once innocent and unencumbered like those dogs and chipmunks. Perhaps as children we were not frauds. But as we became more complex and as our lives demanded more from us, we layered so many extraneous things over top of our purity. We may even have lost some of the ability to feel accurately and to respond in the moment with what would be the appropriate level of emotion.

I think of this process as one of remembering. But that word—re-member—lands on my ears like putting us back together. Like we lost a member—an arm or a leg—and re-membering is putting it back on our body. Re-membering our emotional being might be like rebuilding our fully human selves. So, as we engage in the process of discovery and learning, try thinking of it as re-membering your feeling body.

But in our search for re-membering or re-learning our real feelings, we find that emotions are perhaps even more complicated than we might believe them to be. Sometimes it appears that our feelings are in the driver's seat, as Brené Brown says. Sometimes (maybe often for some of us) our emotions override logic and result in actions that are not inappropriate or even fraudulent but which border on confounding. Here's an example of what I mean.

In the classic Kirk Douglas movie *Spartacus* (1960) there is a scene where the Roman ruler declares that the slaves would be spared their horrible death by crucifixion on the sole condition that they identify the one named Spartacus. Just as Douglas is about to state his identity and accept his fate, another man jumps to his feet and says, "I am Spartacus," and then another, and another, until all one hundred or more of them are all shouting, "I am Spartacus." It is a show of solidarity and a willingness to accept fate out of valor. It is illogical and might not make sense to a more rational mind. But there are many times in my life that I was presented with what might be called a Spartacus Moment where I could either stand up and say, "I am Spartacus," or shy away and take the apostle Peter's stand of, "I don't know him!" Why would these men choose to stand with Spartacus—worse yet, claim to be him, knowing it could mean certain death? What makes you or me choose the illogical (read that as emotionally-driven) path?

Our brains are wonderful organs with a specific purpose at their core: our survival. The human brain has an unfathomable capacity to collect, store, and utilize data. These data can be experiences, facts read or heard along the way, or purely emotional information. Then, what the brain does with this information is continually use it in its core function of survival. In other words, as we enter each new moment, the brain takes in all of our perceptions from our five senses—what we see, hear, feel (both tactile and somatic feelings), smell, and even taste. Then it compares those data points with its vast array of stored data and immediately projects out into the next moment or the emerging future. Essentially (if we were to give it a voice) our brains are saying, "This situation is like that previous one in which the following was the outcome, so therefore I project that will be a high probability of occurring here."

That process is ongoing 24/7 three hundred sixty-five days a year and is amazingly speedy. Literally we experience thousands of those projections, big and small, every hour of our waking day. So when the big issues arise, our brains do not differentiate the gravity of them (to the brain everything is life or death) and just continue to do the same collection-comparison-projection routine. This happens whether we are faced with a job promotion or an invitation to go bungee-jumping. It's no different when we are in the Spartacus moment, except what made that scene particularly poignant was that it wasn't Kirk Douglas standing up. Each of the other men, facing certain execution, chose the path that would lead to death not survival. Why? Why and when do we say "I am Spartacus" and when do we step back and duck?

I have often explained it this way. In the simple analysis, we can think of our brains as three brains in one. The most primitive brain, the medulla—often referred to as our reptilian brain—houses, as I mentioned, our autonomic systems (responsible for breathing and the beating of our hearts, and much more). These autonomic processes are necessary for survival but are also wired into our need to procreate and pass on our genes to the next generation.

The second level of our brain is the cerebrum or what has been referred to as the limbic brain and has often been associated with the seat of our emotions (not necessarily true as we will get into later). It has often been said that what differentiates mammals from reptiles is our care for our young, a thing attributed to our limbic brains. And the third and largest part of our brain is the cortical brain–the cerebellum—all that gray matter we see when looking at a lab specimen. The cerebral cortex is home to our reasoning and logic.

But here's the thing that researchers found: Our lower-level brain functions have the ability to override the higher functions. How many of you have found that despite all the logical reasons not to, we have fallen "stupidly" in love? And worse yet, how many of you have had the need for survival override your emotions or your logic. We do things that don't make logical sense because of our emotions or because of our need for survival. And, yes, that includes sex—sex is a reptilian function and it can overrule emotions and logic at the drop of a hat!

All of those men who stood up in defiance saying "I am Spartacus" were acting on a different level. It was neither a logic-driven statement or a choice for survival but rather one of emotion and personal values. Given the choice of crucifixion, dying as a slave or messing with the powers of the system by all claiming to be that wanted man, they all chose to act in defiance and to disregard their personal consequences. That illogical but emotion/value-driven action is not something we can program into our Artificial Intelligence machines. Values and emotions can cause us to act in unpredictable ways.

> Jeremy had just recently been hired; in fact he hadn't even been in his new role for six months when the SVP in charge of the local office left for another job. The upper management saw potential in Jeremy and approached him with a juicy proposal: Would he consider taking the lead role at this branch (along with the promotion to senior vice president)? Jeremy thought long and hard about it. He was good at his profession, but that was as an individual contributor and as an expert at the craft itself. However, he had never really led a team of people, much less led a team of other professionals. He was curious as to why they would tap him and not one of the other consultants in the office who had been there longer and who knew the ins and outs of the firm's practices. After less than a day of thinking and without asking any other questions, Jeremy said he did not feel ready to take the role and passed on the offer. In a sense, he was saying, "I'm not Spartacus—I don't even know him."

I certainly have had my share of Spartacus Moments, where I was faced with a choice to step into leadership, to lean in to a challenge or push back on the powers that be. For example, back in the days of the Vietnam war, I had entered college intent on going into the military as a chaplain, so I was in ROTC my entire freshman year. But over the summer before my sophomore year we had a week of ROTC "summer camp." One of the classes we had to take was what I called "kill class." It was teaching a series of moves that could kill a person with one single movement—not exactly the *Kill Bill* five finger death punch, but, yeah, stuff like that. At one point the instructor laughed as he was saying, "You have to step to the side when doing this because the blood comes out so fast, heh, heh!" I was repulsed and nauseated. I stood up and said, "Excuse me, sir, but that is disgusting. There is nothing funny about taking a life. I need to leave now." And I walked out of the room and out of the training.

At first, they wanted to charge me with being AWOL from the training (which was somewhat moot since this was only ROTC after all). But then they sent the higher-ranking student officers after me in an attempt to call me back. I had been the highest rank (master sergeant) of the freshman class and showed promise as a leader. All would be forgiven if I would come back for the fall semester. Instead of rejoining ROTC, I became a radical anti-war protester. I wore my fatigue jacket with my name on it so I could be identified at any protest. Perhaps it should have read, "I am Spartacus." I became ROTC's nemesis on campus and a leader of a group called The New Mobilization to End the War (New Mobe for short).

On the other side of things, I have also had my moments of stepping back from the limelight. Some of these will come up in this book: shying away from my path into the ministry, not calling off a marriage I knew I should not have entered, and career moves somewhat similar to Jeremy's. So part of what I will want to dig into is why I would choose the Spartacus or not-Spartacus assessment. Of necessity I will have to look into the role of guilt and shame. I will be faced with questions about my being in touch with (or lack thereof) my emotions and what might be considered "irrational" and emotion-driven decisions. Emotional reactions and emotion-based decisions are by definition not rational or logical. Choosing to stand with Spartacus or choosing not to is more often not in the realm of logic.

Such choices are often emotionally driven choices. There is a feeling that comes over us—seemingly out of nowhere, but in actuality, from our beliefs and values. So it is critically important to dig into our beliefs, values, attitudes, and thoughts that serve as precursors to our emotional reactions or emotionally-based actions. So, as much as we would like to believe that our brains (that is, the cortical brain, at least) are in charge, there are many times when it is not that way. We can be too deliberate and hesitant at one point and then far too impulsive at another. We can get hot-headed when challenged by someone else and result in getting way over our heads or in a fight for our lives we hadn't expected.

And yet, most of the time we make decisions that are well thought out and completely rational. Most likely Spartacus's fellow slaves were not acting with such rationality. They were more likely than not reacting out of an emotional state and not considering the full ramifications of their actions. It makes for a great movie scene but probably won't do much for our long-term survival.

In the classic experiential game called "The Prisoner's Dilemma" people are paired with a random partner they do not know. Each person is given the same set of rules with the object of the game to accumulate the least amount of prison time. Each "prisoner" is being interrogated and has the option of blaming the other person or remaining silent about their guilt. But the dilemma is that neither prisoner knows what the other prisoner will do, and it is only when both persons have given the interrogator their decision will they know the score they receive on that round. And, to further complicate the dilemma, scores are dependent on the combination of both prisoners' statement! The game can also be played with groups of people, making the decision process more complex by requiring a complete vote (majority rules) of all participants. If anyone abstains, the vote cannot be counted.

Playing the game involves both emotional responses as well as calculated logic. In playing the Prisoner's Dilemma, I have actually seen groups get in heated arguments that come close to fighting! But the point is to see how each team or individual will play the game which is based on (spoiler alert) the creation of a win-win scenario. The only way to produce the least amount of jail time is for both parties to cooperate with each other and remain silent about the other's culpability. Similar to the men in Spartacus, the players must sacrifice their own desire to win at the expense of another in order for all to win the game. While there are many variations on the Prisoner's Dilemma, the idea is to see how individual and group decisions are made—selfishly, for self-preservation, or for altruistic values and for the betterment of all.

I look at this challenge from two differing perspectives. First, is the decision-making process. Those of us who were leading the early study on decisions and decision-making, attempted to squeeze emotionality out of the decision. This effort continued well in to the 90s as is evidenced by Antonio Damasio's research reported in his book *Descartes' Error*.[10] Demasio was among the first to argue that the mind and body are inseparable and that the whole system is involved in the decision process. How we make decisions by integrating emotions as part of the "data" we consider in making those decisions is, again, like the top of the iceberg—it is the part above water.

But that second part—understanding the difference between knowing about emotions and fully experiencing them—is the real mass of the iceberg. How do we respond to our emotions or, perhaps more accurately, how do our emotions sometimes override the logic of our rational decision-making process?

Questions to Ponder:

1. How conscious are you of your emotions? Where and when have you been unconscious of what and why you feel?

2. When have you made those emotionally driven choices that might be called Spartacus Moments?

3. What are the times when you have not been living your purpose (fraudulent) and what motivates you to be that way?

---

10. Antonio Damasio, *Descartes' Error* (New York: Penguin/Vintage Books, 1994), reprinted in 2006.

Part Two:
Developmental Pathways

5

When I Am a Hammer

Have you ever noticed that when you think of yourself as a hammer (a problem solver) everything ese looks like a nail? It's certainly true for me. Throughout my life and growing up, I encountered many situations that welded that in place, and from what I can see now, this all started at a much earlier age.

"What are you going to do? Cry about it?" (Kids can be so cruel!)

"I don't like what you are doing; it's not right," I responded, flushed and tearful.

The guys were playing a "game" they called "frog ball" where, instead of using a baseball, they were swinging at, and most often hitting, a live frog with a bat—or at least it was live until the point of impact!

I was angered, embarrassed, disgusted, and probably another ten emotions on top of that. The flood of emotions leaked out of my eyes. In that moment I made two decisions: that these were no longer friends I would hang out with and that my emotions were not to be discussed or even shown outwardly with my peers.

That decision, at about the age of twelve (and perhaps a foreshadowing of the decision to leave ROTC), was just one of many times when I thought the solution was clear and hammered it into place. However, doing so resulted in my being alone for much of the time. We lived in a small rural "neighborhood" with very few other boys I could play with. I had my sports which, irrespective of my being awkward and not very talented, at least offered social interaction of sorts. There were the coaches who pushed us to draw blood from the opponent or like the one who told me to "spit on it and rub it in the dirt." I had to rein in my emotions or at least not wear them on my sleeve. It was one of those hard life lessons—one of many that have formed me at my core. Emotions were messy, got in the way, and furthermore I didn't like these emotionally charged and emotion-based decisions.

What develops and evolves us as humans are stressors, challenges, and problems. We do not develop or grow much by doing something easy or comfortable. In fact, I would be so bold as to say that nothing is ever accomplished by people who want to be comfortable and stress-free. How we handle those stressors and challenges and how we solve our problems are where we grow. That is certainly true for me and my life. As I look at my best skills and those on which I most rely, they were all learned on the back side of some significant hardship, tough experience, or total smack in the head!

When it comes to problem-solving, much the same is true, except that I was taught as a young lad growing up, "If you want something done right, do it yourself"—a saying mostly attributed to Napoleon or the French dramatist *Étienne Jodelle*, but which my dad insisted came from Abraham Lincoln.

This independence, which I thought was a skill or strength, was something like those other great skills referred to above. It came on the heels of a hard hitting "challenge" when my dad died suddenly when I was just eighteen. Growing up, I imagine most of us figure that our parents will always be there for us as guides and mentors—at least until we get into our early adult years. And the fact that my father was only 42 at the time of his death meant that it was not only untimely but shockingly unexpected at the same time. There was no time to prepare. He had not been ill nor did he have some advanced stage of an incurable disease. He had a silent killer–a blood clot that landed in the LAD artery, the most important of the three main arteries supplying blood to the heart muscles, often referred to as "the widow-maker."

My sister and I made all the arrangements and decisions about the funeral and burial. Mom was too much in shock. There was little time to stew about decisions; we just decided and went with it. No problem! But the other side of that expediency was that I never really took time to grieve my father's death in the present moment. It wasn't until I was at freshman orientation a few weeks later, wondering why my hands hurt, that it hit me. We had gone with a military funeral as dad was still active in the army. And as a result, I had felt rather useless. So, at the cemetery, I asked the funeral director how dad was to be buried. He pointed to the backhoe parked a bit down the road, "They just fill it in." I asked if my brother, my best friend, and I could get three shovels, and after everyone left, we began filling the hole. Those first few shovelfuls were painful, but by the time we were finished we were sweating and laughing—it was quite cathartic. The problem of grieving was handled, and again I was a hammer for that nail! My hands were sore because of all of the shoveling, but the pain of my grief had hidden that memory already.

Back to the topic: I have been fascinated by problem-solving and decision-making skills for quite some time. My first formal encounter with decision-making was as a young grad student at Penn State. Along with my advisor and another psychologist on the faculty, we won a grant to develop a textbook on decision-making which resulted in my first book, co-authored with Drs. Karl Bartsch and Elizabeth Yost. Burdened with the dry title of *Effective Personal and Career Decision Making (EPCDM)*,[11] our text was used only in colleges that had freshman orientation courses, so I wouldn't classify it as a best seller! But then again, it was not about the book. What was more important was learning a methodical, logical decision process.

Essentially, we broke out what we called "the anatomy" of the decision into several parts. First, knowing that our alternatives (our choices) are often apples-to-oranges comparisons at best, we taught that instead of comparing the two, three, or more alternative options against each other, we should compare them against what we desire from the decision. These values we called Desired Outcomes, and we had people weight the Desired Outcomes subjectively on a 1-10 basis. This is where "feelings" were to come into the process. It wasn't so much about the feelings one had for the decision itself but how strongly one felt about the various outcomes.

Having first established the outcomes and their relative weightings, we listed the various alternatives to be evaluated. This would form a grid of alternative options or actions across the top with the weighted desired outcomes down the left side. Each intersecting cell then asked the question, "How well does that alternative satisfy this desired outcome?" Answers to those questions were rated as double plus, single plus, neutral, single minus, or double minus (what we called the Probability Estimates). These valences were then multiplied by the weight of the desired outcome for that cell. The columns under each alternative were totaled showing ultimately which alternative satisfied the greatest number of highest weighted desired outcomes. Simple, right?

Perhaps the *EPCDM* project was part of what set me on this path of behaviorism or of turning away from the feelings. We never asked participants about how they felt about their various options. On the contrary we helped them get clear about the relative desirability of specific desired outcomes and about the relative probability of the various alternatives.

---

11. Karl Bartsch, Elizabeth Yost, and Kris Girrell, *Effective Personal and Career Decision Making* (Washington, DC: Westinghouse Learning Corp., 1976).

One student was puzzled, asking, "But doesn't how I feel about the option matter?"

"In a way, yes, and in a way no," Karl answered. "What you feel will help you add a valence to the desired outcomes of the decision, but we would caution you about making emotion-based decisions as your emotions are much more arbitrary and may change from moment to moment."

The student was left scratching his head, still not convinced.

Our premise was that what messed people up in trying to decide among options and alternatives in a very complex decision was not how they felt about one alternative versus another but rather how well each option might fulfill the weighted desired outcome. Confusion, we felt, was the result of our minds jumping about the "grid" created by comparing alternatives to the outcomes, saying, "Well if I do this, then I can get that. But if I do this other one, I would get something else." We essentially took decision-making out of the realm of the emotional and placed squarely in the intellectual realm. Seeing our decisions on paper allowed us some level of objectivity about the decision process. Plus, it also afforded the decider the opportunity to change the weightings or the probability estimates and see how that might change the overall outcome of the decision-making process.

I see that as I was often leaning to a more analytical life, to become more "logical" in my decision process, I had brief flips to the other end of the spectrum. For example, in stark contrast to what I was doing in grad school, I made the highly emotional decision to marry my college sweetheart. She was charming, talented, extremely intelligent, and highly recruited in her field of study, metallurgy. But the attraction and emotions that brought us together were not sufficient to sustain the relationship, especially when my young wife began travelling all over the country with another metallurgist setting up processes and experiments in steel plants and manufacturing facilities. Time away and travel with a young single colleague took its toll and she made the decision to leave me and move in with him.

The pain and suffering of this (and many other such events) ultimately became the catalyst for much of my growth and development, but I will come to that later.

I needed decision-making to be a logical process because, as a young adult, I had not yet learned how to accept and deal with emotional information. I had always identified myself as a deeply feeling, "sensitive" kid, but I had been told that was not good or functional (the frog ball incident was just one of many instances where I eventually learned to suppress my feelings). I kept getting the message that feelings were weak and always coming and going–not a stable foundation for something as important as making an important decision. In fact, I learned that emotions were okay to be experienced but not taken as important. As a result of learning that (who knows where), I felt guilty about my feelings.

Despite being a part of my previously learned self-concept (that is that I was a sensitive person), I learned to discount them, relegate them to some far corner of my being, and in doing so, I became distrustful of my feelings and embarrassed about having them.

At about the same time as we were working on the decision-making process, researchers were looking into negotiation as an element of decision-making. The hotbed of that research was Harvard where only a few years later in 1979 two researchers, Roger Fisher and William Ury founded the Harvard Negotiation Project. Their work, outlined in the now-famous *Getting To Yes*,[12] reduced negotiations to a logical, almost purely economic process. On the other side of this investigation, psychologist Daniel Kahneman and economist Amos Tversky at the University of Chicago were looking at negotiations and decisions from an emotional perspective.[13] Kahneman was responsible for the term "cognitive bias," an effect that the brain has that actually distorts the way we see things. Tversky and Kahneman found that the way a situation was "framed" had a significant effect on decisions and choice. Their research (which won a Nobel Prize) on cognitive bias and the "irrationality" of our thinking speaks to the Spartacus event. It demonstrated that how the situation unfolds and beliefs and feelings that we hold around those events can override the logic.

Apparently, I was not alone in this experienced dichotomy between logic and emotion. We are continually bombarded by advertisements that appeal to our emotional decision-making not our logic. According to Harvard Business School Professor Gerald Zaltman, 95% of our purchase decision-making takes place subconsciously (on the emotional level, not logical).[14] Furthermore, our brains get a bit overwhelmed with too many choices or too much information. Witness, for example, the fact that less than 1% of people doing Google searches ever click through to the second page, despite the banner at the top of the search output that reads "1-10 of 36,000,000 results." I'm not sure whether it is my laziness or my naivete at thinking that these first ten results are the best (as opposed to just what SEO has thrown at me).

Barry Schwartz, another Harvard professor, shows research that when people are presented with a greater number of choices or alternatives, they are less likely to do anything than in situations that present only three options. Schwartz set up tables at a local supermarket with some jellies and crackers, offering a dollar-off coupon if the customer were to buy one of the products. In one market they offered three jellies to sample, while in the other store they offered ten different jellies and jams. Interestingly, over 70% of the customers

---

12. Roger Fisher and William Ury, *Getting to Yes: Negotiating Agreement without Giving In* (New York: Penguin Books, 1981).
13. Daniel Kahneman and Amos Tversky, "Prospect Theory: An Analysis of Decision Under Risk," *Econometrica*, 47, no. 2 (March 1979).
14. Logan Chierotti, "Harvard Professor Says 95% of Purchasing Decisions Are Subconscious," *Inc. Magazine* (March 26, 2018).

who had three samples to try took the coupon and bought one of the jams, but in the stores where there were ten jams and jellies only 3% of the customers bought any.[15]

There was an interesting twist on the emotional decision process when researchers asked about participants' satisfaction with their choices. In a number of studies, it has been repeatedly found that when there appears to be an option to change your mind and make a different decision, those who had no option to renegotiate were more satisfied with their decision than those who had the option to re-choose. Not only were they happier with their choice but when asked to rate their selected option against the other options that had been presented, they consistently rated it more positively than when they were originally presented their choice options.[16] I hear this play out so many times with many of my married male friends.

> Dude: "My wife is getting sloppy and fat, and I am totally unattracted to her."
>
> Me: "Tell me why you got married to her."
>
> Dude: "She was vivacious, young, and always ready for sex anytime we got together. Now she tells me that sex is the furthest thing from her mind."
>
> Me: "What are your thoughts about that?"
>
> Dude: "You know you look online and there are thousands of women and beautiful women—really—who put themselves out there as looking for a hookup. I wish she looked like some of them. Maybe if she looked like that and took care of herself, she'd be more in the mood."
>
> Me: "Sounds like you think it is all of her making. Where are you in all of what's happening?"
>
> Dude: "Aw, c'mon Kris, look at me. I'm in the best shape of my life. I work out. My business is going great. And there are a lot of women who keep asking me if I want to get together."
>
> Me: "What it sounds like to me is that when you compare your wife to them, the contrast makes her look even worse and you have a kind of repulsed reaction. And the more you show that to her the less likely she is to want to care about herself and have anything to do with you."

It wasn't so much that she had a problem but that he was continually comparing her to younger, beautiful women—which had the side effect of kicking her self-esteem to the curb. Were he to see her as his one-and-only choice and close off the comparisons, not

---

15. Barry Schwartz, *The Paradox of Choice: Why More Is Less* (New York: Harper Perennial, 2005).
16. Daniel Gilbert, *Stumbling on Happiness* (New York: Vintage/Random House, 2007).

only would she not feel put down, more importantly he would be looking at her as his love and seeing her inner beauty. As an interesting corollary to this story, shortly after this conversation, his wife was contacted by an old flame who still adored her. They started seeing each other, and in a matter of just a few months she had lost the weight, was dressing up, and felt great about herself. And, not surprisingly, she left the marriage and filed for divorce.

Somehow, all of these "facts" were things that seemed intuitively obvious to me, with the exception of the choice satisfaction data from Gilbert. Just like the "Dude" above, as I was growing up, I always seemed to suffer from "buyer's remorse," second-guessing my choices and decisions. With my childhood backdrop and perpetual second-guessing, it was no wonder that I took to the EPCDM project with such gusto. It made sense to me and it was a way to move through decisions without being overwhelmed by the emotionality of them. And it provided a logical path to reconsidering the options and choices before pulling the trigger on the decision.

But decisions are only one class of problems that needed to be solved. There are all kinds of problems that we encounter every day—from mate selection, to jobs and cars and all the way down to ice cream flavors. Each decision is taken in the face of a choice point: The car broke down and you need to buy another one. How could we make this process more efficient and streamlined? And, as I said, I was always taught to be a problem-solver (a hammer). It didn't matter if it was a crossword puzzle or one of those math word problems (which I particularly enjoyed), problems were fun challenges and not problematic at all. They were all nails that needed my hammer! So when life presented a problem, I always wanted to rise to the occasion.

And I got really good at it. If there was a lab assignment in college, I would take the lead. Researching the background to solving a problem was an adventure. But decision-making and problem-solving were only a small facet of the human experience.

In grad school I started learning about psychological testing (personalities and later behavioral testing). Assessments opened up the world of understanding about personality and the effects of emotions. These were incredibly fascinating, although I first was a bit too literal with my interpretations. In one of the few doctoral study classes I took, specifically, Tests and Measures, the professor gave a final exam that was one sentence long: "Who am I?" it read. She provided six personality test outputs and we were tasked with figuring what character from literature was being represented by the instruments we were provided. Thinking back on that, it was a brilliant exercise to say the least.

I picked the wrong character for all the wrong reasons! I had not interpreted the combination of tests correctly nor had I solved the problem. Gauntlet down! That failure set me on a path of wanting to become one of the best in the business. It is funny how that works! We think little of our successes other than whatever we did worked. However, when it comes to failures, we slice and dice and inspect the daylights out of what we did, could have done, or might have done differently or better.

I started getting really good at test interpretations and was hired for many assessments and feedback sessions. In my latter years as a consultant, I would frequently be sent a test or battery of tests from some colleague across the country who was stumped by the array of data that just didn't seem to fit together. I loved the challenge and especially loved the positive strokes after cracking the code! I could see the connection between personalities, self-concepts, and how people acted.

Over the span of my career, I moved from higher education career planning and placement to corporate outplacement and then into strategic consulting and leadership coaching. Armed with my psychometric talent and penchant for solving problems, I was a natural and found my home helping companies solve their people and leadership problems. As consultants, we don't provide the solutions; we only ask more and better questions, and the tools I had learned for asking better and better questions served that function to a tee.

But none of that translated to my personal life too well. Often, we can build a particular skill in one area of our life and still be in the starting blocks in another.

> "it's not about you," Sarah said through her tears. "I am just telling you how I feel!"
>
> "But you said the word 'you' as in 'When *you* do that, I feel . . .'" I explained, somewhat defensively.
>
> "It's not *about* you, and furthermore there is nothing to fix. I am just telling you how I feel," was her slightly more emphatic retort.
>
> "Well, what do you want me to do with that information?" (now really confused).
>
> "Nothing! Can you please just listen and let me tell you what is going on inside my head?"

Sarah was giving me vital information but was not at all interested in my solving anything. It took me more than a decade of marriage to finally understand how to listen to emotional information in a supportive way (Translation: not seeing the emotions as problems to be solved). Apparently, emotions were not problems!

What I am reporting on here is not simply a male issue. Though, historically, we men have been schooled on the problem-solving mentality. And to add insult to injury, we have not been very well trained on the usefulness or sometimes even the awareness of our emotions.

My friend Andy Chaleff, a masterful coach/consultant, related a similar conversation[17] he had with his wife early on in their relationship:

> Her: "So I am having a problem at work with Billy and I think I should . . ."
>
> Him: "Before you say another word, why don't you simply get rid of him? It's been a long time that you have discussed this and I don't see it going anywhere."
>
> Her: "This isn't really helping."
>
> Him: "Maybe so, but you asked me for my opinion and I am giving it to you."
>
> Her: "I did not want your opinion. I wanted your support."
>
> Him: "Well, this is what my support looks like."

Andy says that his quick mind always assesses the problem and is ready to jump into solution mode ASAP. But what problems often require is deep listening and emotional intelligence. Where he was missing the boat was that his wife had asked for support and he had heard her request as asking for solutions instead. Andy's training was in business process management layered on to a life of emotional awareness. While he had always been seen as aware and sensitive to the needs of others, when a problem popped up, he was the guy you wanted on the team. He was the answer man. All our education and training seem not to matter when we solutions-oriented people are presented with the exciting task of solving a problem.

I certainly had enough education in the field of psychology, but when I was going through college, there was no course on human emotions. In fact even today, a survey of course listings at Penn State University, where I did my undergrad and graduate programs, (looking today at human development and psychology course listings) there is only one course on the topic. The same is true for the University of Maryland where I did coursework toward a doctorate degree. Locally, Northeastern University currently lists a couple of courses on emotions and on affective sciences (kudos to them), MIT only focuses on artificial intelligence, Boston College has none save a few courses on sensation and perception, and the same is true for Boston University. But I would wager that there still are scant few courses that address the subject of emotions. So where are we to learn this?

However, I digress.

The long and short of it is that despite having degrees and studies in psychology, counseling, psychometry, and later even theology, I have never had a formal course that dug into the science of emotions. So maybe I am not so much a fraud as I am just undereducated in this

---

17. Andy Chaleff, *The Connection Playbook: How to Create Deep Harmony Within Yourself and Others* (forthcoming, 2022).

aspect of my life. PSU was a very behavioral school of psychology and really did not ever delve into emotions or affective aspects of human awareness. And while the University of Maryland was more analytic in its psych department's orientation, nothing of the kind was ever discussed there either. So my understanding and awareness of emotions was gleaned from articles and research on the impact of emotions on human behavior.

If I am to understand what emotions and beliefs were at the core of my past behavior, I needed to research further what emotions are and how they work. And that exploration started with this inward journey of reflection and perhaps meditation on the subject. Though I had been introduced to meditation (Transcendental Meditation back in the early 70s), I hadn't practiced it and still had no clue of what meditation was and how it would help me find what I was looking for—something I will discuss later on.

Questions to ponder:

1. How often do you not trust your emotions in decision-making?

2. In interpersonal and relationship situations where do you draw on logic versus drawing on your emotional information? Which seems richer and which seems more reliable to you?

3. How might you improve your ability to savor the emotion and let that emotion percolate with other information?

6

My Four-Legged Stool

From the outset, let me reiterate that I have not been terrifically skilled at remembering or thinking back over my life's experience. Maybe that is because I don't want to remember them, but I always believed that it is because I tend to be strategic and very forward-thinking. At least that is the story I would tell myself.

"When you got divorced from your first wife," she asked in all earnestness, "what was it like for you?"

"I think I tried to blot that all out," I replied. "It was a terrible time, and I don't remember much of it. Or at least I don't want to remember much of it."

"Well then, what about your second marriage—at least that is a bit more recent?" she continued, undaunted by my lack of specificity.

"Oh that—that I refer to that as the 'dark times,'" I answer. "I really can't make sense of dates and times or events even to this day."

And it is the truth. Thinking back to the events surrounding the demise of my second marriage and the years following it, I know I lived in four different places, but the dates don't add up and I cannot, for the life of me, remember where and when things happened. Just snippets and a few photographs.

Was it that I didn't want to relive the negativity of those highly emotional days, or was I avoiding something that I needed now to unpack and from which I could learn? Had I really blotted them out with alcohol and sex or were they just buried under layers of guilt and shame? What was it that I was avoiding? What was at the core of what happened, or what was I the cause of that was just too ugly to look at?

To totally deconstruct what our resistance to feelings is made of, we may have to start back in the beginning. What shaped you and how were your core self-concepts formed? While our family of origin shapes some of that foundation up through the age of, let's say, six or seven, once we become part of a peer cohort, our social interactions with our band of brothers or sisters kicks into full power.

We hear this regularly at the early childhood education center (preschool) my wife runs. Some of the children spend their first years at home under the care of a grandmother or au pair. But shortly after they begin attending our school, the parents come in saying how fast their child has learned vocabulary, manners, interaction skills, and topics even they knew little about. Interacting with a class of 18 or 19 other children has a multiplicative effect. So it is more often the case that we have learned much if not most of what we know about ourselves in relationship with others. We are social creatures and live within social structures called cultures. In exploring cultures, I want to look at the culture as a context but not as a unified whole. Rather, culture can be thought of as our social culture (socio-economic culture), our religious culture, our formal education as a cultural training, and—for me, this was really influential—through music as culture. I think of it as a kind of four-legged stool.

In order to better understand my emotions and the emotional backdrop to my various behaviors, I needed to explore the roots of my being; how I came to see myself and how my core beliefs about myself and my world were influenced by these various cultural elements. How was my four-legged stool constructed? Growing up and from a very early stage of growing up, I noticed (or at least had the thought) that I was different from the other kids. I liked reading; they liked cars and climbing trees. When other kids were drawing planes or race cars in art class, I was sketching out floor plans for fantasy houses. Gradually I became more of a loner with only three real buddies in those formative grade-school years.

How had that happened and what was the root system underpinning it all? It was time to go *digging in the dirt* and trying to unearth those roots. A song called Digging in the Dirt by Peter Gabriel speaks to this. The lyrics in part say it is only in finding those dark places that are hidden in the humus, where all dead things have composted that we will find not only the things that hurt us but be able to locate their source and effects.[18]

Socialization and Culture. How exactly has your culture informed you and how you think of yourself? As I look back, I first must recognize the culture from which I came. We

---

18. Peter Gabriel, "Digging in the Dirt," Geffen Records, 2006.

lived in subsistence—not abject poverty, but we could see it from there. I can remember that Wednesday nights were oatmeal night—that was dinner, just oatmeal. And Friday was always spaghetti. Mom and dad did what they could to make the money last from paycheck to paycheck and we three kids didn't really know the difference between us and others, or even that we were poor. But in retrospect, that is what it would be called: subsistence. The ethics that come from that world of poverty are mixed. Of course, there were the salt-of-the-earth values of loving and respecting your neighbors. We were taught that we should always give of what we had and that we could learn from anyone— that everyone had value, just for who they were. We were also taught to respect all life and nature itself as the source of life.

> My grandfather was a jack-of-all-trades, but mostly he approached everything as a learning experience. Nature was a kind of temple for him, and he would teach lasting lessons on wild-harvesting foods like nuts, berries, and mushrooms. But he was also a fine wood worker. Every time we were around him as he was building something, he would call us over. "C'm'ere, c'm'ere," he'd say as he held the two pieces of wood together where it was cut. Then he would slowly expose the cut to us and, in almost a whispered voice, as if it were magic or something extremely sacred, would say softly, "No one has ever seen this before!" It truly was a magical moment. He taught us that everything was living (even rocks), everything was sacred, and everything had a lesson to teach.

But beneath the surface, not too deeply buried in the dirt, there were other subtle messages of the culture, some of which have taken a lifetime to extract. For instance, somewhere I learned that all I had of value was me —my body—and all the rest, all of those material things, did not matter. There were good things about that. I learned to work hard and to give myself physically to every effort, whether it was helping a neighbor move or digging a ditch to help the drainage in the area. I was told that God gave me a big body and strength so that I could be of use to others. But what wasn't present, at least from what we perceived at the lower rungs of the economic ladder, was a sense of future. There was a subtle message that you dare not hope for a brighter future because there was no escape from this. This was life and you'd better accept it. There was no stability in subsistence living. People were jerked around by circumstances and the unpredictable nature of life was more amplified for poorer people.

But the dark side of that physicality contained a sexual overtone. All I had to offer was my body—but that was something I could use. That was also something the girls would use as well. Somewhere in the recesses of po' folk morality is the thought that money is nothing (or worse, it was evil), but your body—as in your sexual being—was something that mattered. Even if you didn't have a dime, you could still give yourself physically or receive sexually from others. People living in the lower fringes of society learn that sex is a currency that mattered and that could and would be used either to get something you needed (shelter, relationship, and even money) or simply as a means of finding an escape—escape from this dead-end life or literally escape, like some form of relief, in the moment.

And it was the escape clause that most of us focused on. But what does the research say about the relationship of rural morality and sexual exploration? To be clear, I am not talking about the stereotypical Appalachian image of an ignorant, bucktoothed man or of a white "trailer trash" person or Daisy Duke type of woman. While the area I came from qualifies as Appalachia, it by no means fit the cartoon stereotype of a hillbilly backwoods low life. To the contrary, our town had the full strata from relatively wealthy to those of subsistence level poverty. Nonetheless, there were certain elements of the mythos of Appalachia that applied. Sex and marriage presented some sort of stability (at least we have each other to hold on to in this crazy ride of life) and partnership in dealing with the challenges. Judith Fiene's study of Appalachian young women found that the bulk of young women's dreams centered around their future role as a family maker and that their sexual explorations were all aimed at finding the most suitable partner who would provide that stability.[19] Another study contrasting rural and nonrural adolescents found that rural teens are both more likely to engage in sex and that they lose their virginity at an earlier age than their urban counterparts.[20] [21] [22]

While sex was a perhaps passage into marriage or a passport out of the territory, it remained a central focus of a lot of people on the lower levels of the society. And sex was not fraught with any upper-class morality—it was free and available. Again, music chimes in from the back recesses of my memories—this time from Mungo Jerry and a song called *In the Summertime*.[23] Generally, the song says that the rich folk have a set of ethics and rules that you would need to follow in dating but that if you are poor, the rules are suspended and you can do whatever you want.

I don't believe that Mungo Jerry meant simply that you could stay out late! Rich people could wait and could look to the future, but poor folk had only the now, so "use it or lose it," as they say! You can also hear the same morality in some of the older country & western songs. The themes were obvious. Something like, "We don't have anything, but we have this—this moment, this passion, this one sexual act." I don't know where I picked

---

19. Judith Ivy Fiene, "The Social Reality of a Group of Rural, Low-Status Appalachian Women: A Grounded Theory Study, (PhD diss., University of Tennessee, 1988), https://trace.tennessee.edu/utk_graddiss/4033.

20. Cheryl S. Alexander et al., "Early Sexual Activity among Adolescents in Small Towns and Rural Areas: Race and Gender Patterns," *Family Planning Perspectives 21*, no. 6 (Nov. - Dec., 1989): 261-266.

21. Robin R. Milhausen et al., "Rural and nonrural African American high school students and STD/HIV sexual-risk behaviors," *American Journal Health Behavior* 27, no. 4 (July-August 2003): 373-9, https://pubmed.ncbi.nlm.nih.gov/12882431/.

22. Shyamal Kumar Das, Asharf Esmail, and Lisa Eargle. "Men's Exploration of Multiple Sexual Partners: Economic vs Psychosocial Explanation," *Bangladesh e-Journal of Sociology* 6, no. 1. (2009), https://citeseerx.ist.psu.edu/viewdoc/download?doi=10.1.1.500.5187&rep=rep1&type=pdf.

23. Mungo Jerry, "In the Summertime," Union Square Music, 1970.

that up, but I know for a fact that physicality, including sexuality, was seen as a survival factor to be reckoned with. We all had *that*, at least. And I saw how it played out in luring in and catching a mate (a sign of stability and hope for some) and as a way of escaping this impoverished, backwoods hole we called home.

It was a mixed message. As I grew from a wimpy nerd into a large, strong male (varsity tackle, wrestler, and such), I felt that had much to offer physically, and I felt good about that. But everything I had learned about sexuality was discovered in the woods, out behind the stadium, and in dark places where you didn't talk about it. It was a Bob Seger world that he talked about in his song, *Night Moves*,[24] and on the heels of that, *Fire Down Below*.[25] Ah, that was my world, and I took it to heart. I viewed dating as practice and would, of course, try to practice as often as I could. So, obviously, I need to consider the effects that music had on my "upbringing."

Music as Socialization. Judging from the cues in the previous section, you might say that music played a big part in how I came to experience my world. Music was always there painting pictures of something different or somewhere else. And music became my teacher—as it was and has been for all people across time.

Music was my heartbeat. Something I discovered later was that many songs were set to sixty beats per minute which is the average pulse rate of most human beings (or double time to quicken our excitement). Perhaps that is why it was so captivating to me because I could feel its rhythm in my pulse. It stirred me. But my parents often joked that I had a movie sound track playing in me because I was always humming some nonsensical tune—it was my internal music.

Music, as a human function, dates back as far as 40,000 years, according to some research, with drawings of instruments like drums and flutes appearing around 35,000 years ago. As humans gathered into communities, evidence of their music-making is clearly evident, right there alongside their pots, utensils, and other artifacts.

And the tones came right from our own bodies in the form of our humanoid vocalizations. Though it wasn't until somewhere around 1500 BCE that the first musical score was written down in a type of cuneiform text, clearly, we humans have been singing and dancing to music since our very beginnings. Rhythm—specifically percussion—and vocalization were tribal ways of communicating, celebrating, and remembering historical events of the tribe. So music became a way in which customs were communicated, relationships were enhanced, rituals were enacted and codified, and rites of passage were celebrated.

Sacred texts like the Hindu Vedas and Persian and Assyrian texts all describe music and its central role in the culture. The function of music was not simply to bring the people

---

24. Bob Seger, *Night Moves*, Capitol Records, 1976.
25. Bob Seger, *Fire Down Below*, Capitol Records, Gear Publishing Company Inc, 1976.

together but perhaps as important as ensuring the survival of the tribe and its culture. More apropos of this book's topic, music is emotional and a means of sharing those emotions. Music bonds us together, in other words, through our shared experiences and feelings. In doing so, it tells our story. In no way is this meant to be an accurate portrayal of music history, but some of the themes that marked music's developmental path are as follows.

Like any art form, musicians toyed and experimented with the creation of different sounds, instruments, progressions, and meters. But let's fast forward a half dozen millennia or so to the modern era and the precursors of today's music. A part of that experimental growth became the birth of the blues and its cousin jazz—both a result of the merger of spiritual songs of enslaved people and the deep-rooted rhythmic tones of African music. Blues had an identifiable rhythm and a message straight from the heart, a message of love and heartbreak. Jazz was that artful experimentation with the form of the same music. Around the same time society went through a crazy period of booming expansion, and to celebrate its freedoms, boogie-woogie and swing burst onto the scene. And then something amazing happened—electronics. We could record not only those sounds but we could alter them electronically and produce new sounds and instruments. Whether you credit Chuck Berry or Les Paul or their musical grandpa, Robert Johnson, rock and roll was born.

And so was I.

Being more or less a loner from my younger years, I listened to a lot of radio when I wasn't in school or curled up with a book. And music, in particular rock and roll, became a type of teacher. Growing up in the late 50s and 60s, rock and roll was just emerging from the world of ballads and blues. The rhythm moved me, to be sure, but the lyrics did even more. Buried in the combination of music and my social environment were the roots of how I began to formulate this identity that I now see as my earlier self-concepts.

The music of the 60s was still innocent—I Want to Hold Your Hand, Let's Get Together—but then the Stones stepped over the line with Let's Spend The Night Together, a line they had to change to perform on the Ed Sullivan Show. For that show the line became "let's spend *some time* together." Then The Kinks came out with Lola and the floodgates were opened. Rock 'n' roll became juicy and sexy—for the most part, that is. What the late 60s began came into full bloom in the 70s. Rock bands flaunted their sexuality[26] and their music was nothing short of explicit. This combined with the sexual revolution and a more prolific use of drugs, from pot to LSD and more, which birthed the 70s mantra, "Sex, Drugs, and Rock and Roll." Since dad was no longer around to teach me about relationships, I was schooled by rock. So, let me start with the sixties.

---

26. Jim Morrison of the Doors was actually arrested for masturbating on stage while singing "Gloria."

I listened to the lyrics and what was being described as a relationship and gathered in those seeds to plant in the compost of my brain. Let's just name a few of the seeds that got planted:

- *Satisfaction* (Stones)
- *Cherry Hill Park* (Billy Joe Royal)
- *Lay Lady Lay* (Bob Dylan)
- *The Lemon Song* (Led Zepplin)

Female singers kept it a bit cleaner for a while, but the boys of rock went straight for the gusto—to see how far they could push the sexual boundaries of public music. Eventually the female "girl bands" would catch up in the 70s with groups like the Bangles, The Waitresses, Joan Jett and company, and so many more. Stories of the Bangles sex orgies on the road, while not making headlines in *Rolling Stone,* at least caught my attention!

That was my world. I could escape with my intellect or I could escape with sex, but that was it until I found my soul in music. And I had to escape. I knew staying there in the "sticks" of western Pennsylvania would be the death of me. And fortunately, God gifted me with enough intellect to make it academically. But it was not before some of those other more sexually-oriented lessons and "values" had been instilled—thanks to rock and roll.

Formal Education as Socialization. Freshman year was a bust, however. High school was never even a challenge but skating by on raw talent alone was not enough to survive college. If freshman year was a bust, sophomore year was an abomination and ended with the psychology department "suggesting" that perhaps this was not the field for me.

"How could you flunk "Ole Soft-touch Hall's class?" my advisor, George, asked. "He's one of the easiest graders in the department."

"I guess I just don't understand how to learn this stuff," was the best retort I could muster.

"Perhaps if you looked at his book not as a class, but for how you might learn how to learn, it might make more sense," Dr. G explained.

That course was entitled The Psychology of Learning, and being the bright kid that I thought I was, I figured that if I could not pass a course in learning, perhaps I did not know how to learn. That summer I read and re-read Hall's textbook. Anything that connected with my style of learning I devoured. I learned what affected memory and recall. I learned about circadian rhythms (a real "aha" since I always had known myself as a morning person, but when studying with the other guys after dinner, I had always just fallen asleep!) and I learned how to learn in a way that it stayed accessible in my brain.

The result was amazing. I started getting straight A's from then on. I wasn't any smarter, but I had learned how to learn and recall. In addition I had moved off campus to a house of other pre-seminary guys. We were serious students and all headed into the ministry. Learning actually became fun. It didn't matter if it was philosophy, advanced psychology, or even Greek (a prerequisite for seminary in those days); I dug in and mastered subjects with gusto. And after graduation, I entered seminary, but I was not ready (read that as not mature enough) and dropped out after just one semester (that is another story).

But there was another part to college and that was the socialization. College is a period of time when young people try on the roles of adulthood. It is a time of experimentation and change. Scholastics are all fine, but living among 50,000 other young people all of whom were changing, challenging and growing along similar lines was spectacular. There were the events and groups on campus and an entire other set of people and events off campus, all just ripe for an explorer like me (and the other 49,999 peers).

On campus there were the dorm rats—people who stayed in their rooms and occasionally went to the dining hall or campus center but not much else. On the up side there were dorm-related social activities and there were dances and concerts every weekend. Who could resist that? But the downside of campus life was noisy, cramped, and not terribly much private space.

The book *The Harrad Experiment* had come out just a few years earlier, but Penn State, where I entered college, had just begun allowing visitation hours (two hours on Sunday afternoon) of opposite sex visitors. Like *The Catcher in the Rye*, *The Harrad Experiment* was almost obligatory reading for students of the sixties and it planted wildly exciting ideas in our minds. The question on everyone's mind was how would we develop differently if we were to be allowed to develop in relationship together?

To provide a little context, Harrad College was a fictional private endowed college that decided to try not simply having coed dorms but actually assigning coed roommates. Roommates were carefully screened and paired based on a number of psychological and sociological factors—but not in the way you might suspect. Students were paired with partners that were almost polar opposites in an effort to force them to break out of confined "pair-bonded" couples and into a more libertine way of being. Social activities were structured so that the pairs would first learn how to be with the opposite sex and then learn how to generalize that out to all of the students at the school.

So you might say that while college was a time of formal classroom education, it was also a stewpot of socialization and sexual education. Nonetheless, the essence of the college experience is diversity. Often for the first time, students are placed in close living situations with individuals and groups with whom they had little exposure before. Through our continual exposure to other groups and peoples, we move from a defensive posture (they just aren't like us), through a stage of minimizing the differences to focus on our similarities, to ultimately accepting the differences as their unique beauty and learning how to adapt to (not just tolerate) those differences and become able to move fluidly between different groups and classes of people.[27]

> On my floor was a classmate who came from Pittsburgh by the name of Tom Brown. Tom was African-American and someone I saw as "cool" and whom I tried to befriend. Having been taught growing up that everyone is equal and worthy, I would try to talk with him but he would always rebuff me.
>
> "Don't Uncle Tom me!" he would say with a mixture of disdain and compassion.
>
> I still didn't get it. "What do you mean—I don't understand that term used in that way!"
>
> "You're just being nice to me *because I am black* not because you want to know *me.*"
>
> "But I do want to get to know who you are—I mean other than a suite mate."
>
> "Then you get to understand my life and what I have to go through. I don't want to be your friend so you can feel righteous about having a black friend—fuck that! If you want to know me, then sit down and shut up and let me tell you what it is like to be a big black man like me. It ain't no picnic!"

That was a more powerful learning experience than 90% of my classes. The same was true of homosexuality later on when I moved off campus. My roommate, Peter, was flamboyantly gay and from time to time would hit on me. This was in the early 70s when people were very cautious about their gayness because they could be beaten up by homophobes. I became Peter's accomplice and somewhat of a bodyguard. One day we had the inevitable conversation.

> "So tell me why you chose to be gay," I asked, always the curious type.
>
> "How tall are you, Krissy?" (he was the only one other than my sister who could get away with calling me that).
>
> "Seriously, I want to know," I said rather frustratedly.
>
> "And I am telling you—how tall are you?"
>
> "I'm six three, why?"

---

27. Mostly this description would be attributed to the work of Milton Bennett but was something I learned from one of my all-time greatest teachers, Lee Knefelkamp.

"Did you choose to be six three?"

"Of course not. I just grew that way," I said.

"Well I didn't choose to be gay, my friend. I just grew that way."

College is that type of a milieu. It is rich with people, places, and things that stretch your boundaries, your self-perceptions and your experiences. And the sixties and seventies were especially rife with those experiences. There were also the missed opportunities.

The year was 1969—the summer of love. I was a camp counselor in southern Connecticut. One of my college suite mates had an internship at General Foods in Tarrytown, New York, and I had a chance to visit him one weekend I had off. Over dinner he asked what I was doing the following weekend—I hadn't any plans.

> "Here take these," he said handing me two tickets. "They're for a rock concert next weekend. General Foods is sending me to New Orleans to see a new plant, and I can't go."

> "Who's playing?" I asked.

> "I dunno," Adrian said, "A couple of good bands." So I took the tickets. But because we counselors didn't get two weekends off in a row, I gave them to a girl counselor I knew on the other side of the lake.

> She never made it back to camp, and to this day I wonder how my life would have been different had I gone to Woodstock instead of her.

These moments, events, and people each form us without our knowing. While I do not assume that you have had similar experiences during your years from 18-24, what I do know is that each of us has come to define a part of who we are and what we know ourselves to be because of the experiences during those powerfully formative years. College—no matter if it was a megaversity or a small college tucked somewhere in among the bucolic hills of some rural state—has formed us and shaped us by the diversity of people and experiences we had there.

Religion as Socialization. Like music, religion—or the wonder and curiosity about things greater than we are— has been a human endeavor since the beginning of recorded time. From cave dweller's art to the very first texts, the themes of God and spirituality (which for all intents and purposes is the inner quest to come closer to oneness with that higher being) have taken a central role in defining who we are. Religion was, at first, very tribal and tribe-specific. We each had our own God and My God could beat Your God. The ancient tribal God was war-like and vengeful. You had better behave for fear of the "wrath of God" that would be visited on you if you weren't.

But as much as religion brought us together, it also did this through a system of out-grouping the "others" and by making them bad or evil. Vestiges of that same mentality still exist today as each fundamentalist group continues to vilify any other belief system while trying to convert them to their own. But for me I had always been perplexed by this paradox. How could a practice that purports to be about love and acceptance, whose sole function was supposed to be about binding us together, be the foundation of wars, hatred, and killing?

As more or less a counterpoint to those lessons of my physical/sexual beingness I learned from music, education, and society were these lessons I learned in church. I had always been attracted to—no, really it was a sheer fascination with—religion. It had so many layers to it and I, being the curious lad that I was, needed to know the whole story. There were the lessons of the scriptures. Not just the ones that were repeated each year on the given date or liturgical festival but the entirety of the scriptures. I read and re-read the Bible—completely, from cover to cover—at least a half dozen times. It was rich with lessons but also rife with juicy stories.

Perhaps you know of how King David lusted for Bathsheba but that he had her husband Uzziah sent to the battle front and purposely abandoned in battle, so he would be killed, thus freeing the now-pregnant Bathsheba for his own. But have you ever read the story of the traveler who was welcomed into the house of a stranger? When the men of the tribe heard of his presence, they called on the host to send him out so that the townsmen could "have their way with him." Instead, they sent out his concubine who was so savagely raped that she was found naked and dead at the doorstep in the morning. (Read Judges 19). As if that were not enough, they then proceeded to cut her body into twelve pieces and send them to the other tribes as a warning. Now that's not a lesson you would ever hear in Sunday school!

Of course, those stories were sources of embarrassment and shame for me. We weren't supposed to read that! But there they were in black and white on the very same pages that were so revered by the elders of the church. We weren't to read them because the church claimed that the entirety of the Bible was the "word of God" and that clearly was not—they were the stories of the history writers and chroniclers of the people. This duality of sacred and profane, of good and sexually evil, and of the divine versus human was welded into place as well. It took its place alongside my other socialization. Your body was created by God—so it was good, right? But sex was part of that same body and yet somehow it was branded as not good. That may have been enough to confuse a young lad like myself, but it didn't. Instead it fueled my curiosity and, by extension, my explorations even further.

The bottom line was that deeply planted at the base of my self-concept was an awareness of my sexuality which was good for many things but at the same time was a source of guilt and shame that was to be hidden from sight. Back when adolescence came upon us all like a thunderstorm on a hot summer night, we began to explore this thing called sexuality. We "used" each other (a few girls in the area and me or some of the other boys I had heard from), and while that felt good and smelled great, it would be hidden, not discussed, and apropos of this discussion, a source of shameful pleasure for me. But it certainly was not something I would ever discuss with dad or mom, or my buddies for that matter. And definitely not something that I would ever think of at church— thank goodness I was not Catholic and required to confess. I didn't want to drag my adventures and discoveries out into public domain and certainly didn't want to soil the reputation of the few willing girls in question—at least not the way I heard the other boys talking about their ventures into sexuality.

So perhaps another clue in this puzzle came through religion. While I consider religion to be one of the four legs of that stool, it was time to look more closely at my religion of origin and my religious explorations to see how they may have shaped what was going on under the surface and its role in guilt and shame.

Questions to ponder:

1. How did you learn your identity—the signature experiences that formed your self-concept?

2. When you are thinking of the experiences that you tried to hide or were told were anywhere from "not right" to shameful, what still lies sleeping in the recesses of your mind?

3. How do you separate what you have learned about yourself and who you say you are?

7

A Backdrop of Religion

If guilt and shame were that prevalent in one part of my socialization, I began to wonder how it might be part of other elements. Certainly, it might explain why I could not remember—or, more accurately, why I chose not to remember certain events. But where did I pick up all the shame stuff? Why had religion become the home of the morality police? Where did all of that shaming originate?

"Dad, why are all these hymns so depressing?" My son and I were in a Lutheran church one Sunday.

"Well, look at the date it was written," I instructed.

"1658," he answered. "What's the significance of that?"

"Well, back then, religion was a part of philosophy, and the philosophers of the time were still trying to figure out why the plague happened."

"But that was in the 1380s." (Pretty sharp for a then 12-year-old!)

"Yes, but it took several hundred years both to recover from it and then to start trying to sort it out. One of the main philosophers of the time was Thomas Hobbes who wrote this incredible tome called *Leviathan* in which he contends that human nature was flawed and that religion really only existed to keep us in line. Martin Luther was very influenced by Hobbes and so that was reflected both in his theology and his hymns."

I had grown up in a Lutheran community and my early years had been heavily imprinted by Lutheranism. Lutherans (mostly of Germanic heritage) were both very stoic and rather depressed. The pews were hardwood and had no cushions, which I suppose only added to their dour expressions and stoicism. Whatever the case, those hymns were part and parcel of our lifestyle.

I started studying Luther when I was young and learned more than what was in his "Small Catechism." Luther had a curious idea which he called *die Anfechtungen*—the trials or temptations. He believed that we were doomed beings and that we were always being put to the test. The only problem was that you could never tell whether the *Anfechtungen* were tests from God or temptations from the devil. This torment infected all of his theology. Like Hobbes, Luther believed that we were basically flawed and forsaken beings. We could do nothing to save ourselves. Only God had the power to do that, and even though Luther believed that God had sacrificed his [sic] son to atone for our sinfulness, there was still nothing we could do to make things right.

Hence, we had those depressing hymns. We were worms, unworthy worms at that. It was not a particularly compelling or enrolling theology. But that was where I started on this journey. I started exploring other religions, kind of like trying on clothes in a store, just to see if anything fit. Though bits and pieces here and there did land, no one religion seemed to capture whatever it was that had me searching for meaning. My Presbyterian friends said that dancing and particularly, rock 'n' roll music were sinful—and I didn't even dare to talk to their moms about Elvis!

Guilt and shame were embedded in nearly all of the major religions—Catholicism, Judaism, Seventh Day Adventists—almost all of them. It was part of how I had begun to understand my world, but somehow it did not make sense. After all, life was good—wasn't it?

Life complexities fouled the water to the point where organized religion had no ready answers and I had to find my own way from there. In the final days of my senior year in high school, war broke out in the Middle East and my church youth group decided to hold a prayer vigil. Fortunately the Six-Day War ended the vigil but not before I had a life-changing experience.

It was the fifth day of the war and I had the overnight shift of the vigil. By three or so in the morning, I had read every prayer and Psalm in the hymnal and had run out of things to say to whatever deity might be listening. I fell into a sort of wordless and thoughtless state. It was still and silent in the church when I felt a sudden cool breeze against my neck. I looked around to see where the draft might be coming from but saw no opened door or window. Then this strange thing happened—thoughts, words, or something I imagined sounded like a voice landed in my ears or possibly in my mind. I "heard" that voice saying. "I want you to teach them about *me*."

"What? Who said that?"

"Teach them; lead my flock."

I am certain, in retrospect, that it was in my head, but it had a sound to it like a voice. And, just like that, it was gone. Every hair on the back of my neck was standing up. In fact, every hair on my arms as well. I had goose bumps all over. What had just happened? Whose voice had I heard? Was this some kind of religious experience? And what on earth was I to do about it?

The next morning I went into the pastor's study and told him what had happened. He said he thought it was a "calling" to the ministry, but that only I could discern that. (I had to look up the word, as I had never heard of discernment before.) At home I told my dad with whom I had had several career/life discussions about going into the military like he did. "Well, now what do you think you'll do?" he asked. I thought for a minute and said that perhaps I would still go into ROTC in college but follow a route into the chaplaincy instead. It was to be the last discussion about life we would have before he died.

So, how do you discern the will of God—does God even have a will (which seemed to me to be a rather human trait)? For me it was a long and winding road through several colleges and a few jobs. So there existed this polarity in me about religion: I felt "called" to some spiritual direction, but at the same time I was learning from my tours through various forms of religious practices that they all had some vestige of guilt and shame woven into their teachings and that just did not fit.

They all taught that sex was for procreation alone and to be experienced only within the container of marriage and at that, in the confines of a dark bedroom. It was not to be discussed, and it certainly was not to be enjoyed. But the bottom-line message of even the so-called sacred act of procreation was that we were all "conceived in sin"—sex was a sin.

That was a killer, because hadn't I enjoyed my little explorations in sexuality? In sexuality I had found beauty. I was beginning to find a level of relationship and a kind of intimate communion that was far beyond anything I had learned in school or from any of my socialization. How was it, then, that both religions and society had made it taboo, dirty, sinful, and unmentionable? I began to wonder if there was a religion that revered and honored sexuality. But I knew it was not Lutheranism, Catholicism, or Methodism—the few with which I had the greatest familiarity.

Brené Brown speaks into the source of guilt and shame in society. First, she distinguishes between guilt and shame as different concepts—not two related on some continuum. Shame, she says, is thinking, "I am bad," whereas guilt is the thought that "I did something bad." Unfortunately, my world had instilled both in me and as I began examining the topic, it appeared that I had blended the two into one bucket! I *was* bad because my religion of origin had taught me that I was fundamentally flawed and not good—and that I had no hope of redeeming myself through my own efforts. Only by the grace of God could my flawed character be restored! And I *had done* bad things by hitting that boy with a brick and by engaging in sexual explorations before the age of consent (and liking it). That was a double whammy.

I sense that I am not alone in those experiences. Many churchgoers had been taught the same lessons. In fact, it was common back in the sixties for Protestants (and pre-Vatican II Catholics) to be taught that we were flawed and helpless. Shame was almost a central tenet of most Christian traditions. But so was guilt prevalent in most of those religions and, as my Jewish wife informs me, of Jewish culture as well. People were taught to "fear" God who, being all-knowing, would know of your wrongdoing.

But Brown also contends that the difference between guilt and shame also is in how they are remedied. Shame can only be healed by learning that we are not dirty, flawed, or evil. In fundamentalistic religions that is called "being saved." We took solace in the Psalms, "Cleanse me with hyssop, and I will be clean; wash me, and I will be whiter than snow." (Ps 51:7).

Guilt, on the other hand, carries within it its own remedy. We cannot actually feel guilt unless we see that something we have done is held in contrast against a backdrop of understanding of what is right. You cannot feel guilt unless you know what you should have done or should want to do, and therefore, knowing what to do to remedy it. Guilt, Brown says, is adaptive and, in a way, developmentally helpful. Shame is destructive and painful.[28]

Brown's research also shows that shame is highly correlated with addiction, depression, violence, aggression, and eating disorders. Holy smokes! I can see parts of each of those in me. She contends that shame often comes from the "I'm not enough" feeling which can either be a result of what we learned as children or have a later onset in midlife as we start evaluating what we have or have not done. As she says, in one TED talk, "I'm just forty-one and what have I accomplished?" We start asking ourselves if we have lived our lives to the fullest potential. And when the answer is on the negative side of the scale, it triggers a kind of depression or acting out as a midlife crisis.

But the question is what happens when we carry both guilt and shame? Do they feed into each other? Brown says that they are separate and distinct and should be treated as such. Shame is about the self and guilt is about the behavior. For women, says Brown, shame "is this web of unobtainable, conflicting, competing expectations about who we are

---

28. Brown, *Daring Greatly*.

supposed to be." She continues, however, saying that for men shame is singular—"do not be perceived as weak!"[29]

But Dr. Brown, at one point in her research, had not yet studied men and their relationship with shame. When confronted by a man one day at a book-signing, she learned of men's different plight. The man told her that his wife and daughters would rather see him die on top of his white horse than watch him fall down. She found in subsequent research (that included men) that it wasn't just the coaches and dads who had instilled this sense of shame in men, but rather it was far more often the women in their lives (the mothers, girlfriends, and wives) who held them to that high standard. That was certainly my experience as well. Women, who have been steeped in that pressure cooker of unobtainable perfection, would heap the same standards on the men in their lives, as was certainly the case in my history. As Brown said in that same TED talk, "Show me a woman who can sit with a man in real vulnerability and fear, and I'll show you a woman who has done incredible work."

I know from my own experience that I had somehow blended them into one self-concept. From the history of my family, religion, and lower-class socialization, I carried bits and pieces of both guilt and socialized shame. I can understand that guilt carries within it its own solution: Start doing more of what we know to be the right thing—the real "us/me." Shame, on the other hand, requires some deep work. Here, Brown contends, the solution is to practice vulnerability—and that is a tall order for the shameful among us. How do we switch from trying to cover up that about which we feel shame by exposing that very same thing?

If there is one other underlying motive for writing this book beyond Sarah's persistent prodding, it is that! Weaving my own history and experiences into the discussion of emotions and emotional intelligence is a very vulnerable act. Just like standing on a TED stage and telling the world that I had my guts ripped open by a massive business failure was an exercise in vulnerability, this book-writing project is one step larger. When I stepped off the stage that day, I had a sick feeling in the pit of my stomach. "What had I just done?" I thought. "I just stood in front of 600 people and admitted that I had failed miserably at business. What if 1,000 people see the video?" I called it my Brené Brown moment (as she once confessed to have had the same feeling after her first TED talk). I think I would have been a lot sicker had I known it was to be viewed so many times.

So with the combination of these formative experiences, I (and again I don't think I am so unique in this) had a slim arsenal of emotions and emotional words to describe them. There was a ton of guilt and shame, laden with the inability to express other emotions that as yet had no names. There were only a few emotions I could draw on from the school of

---

29. Brown, TED. (2012) Listening to shame [Video]. https://www.ted.com/talks/brene_brown_listening_to_shame?language=en

masculinity: happiness, anger and numbness. And, of course there was love—who hasn't experiences that?

> **Questions to Ponder:**
>
> 1. If you had a religion of origin, what morals did it teach you? If not, where did you learn your morals?
>
> 2. What is the difference between your spirituality and your religion (or if not yours, the ones you have heard of)?
>
> 3. What role do guilt and shame play in your overall self-concepts?

8

Moral and Ethical Development

As we discussed in the previous section on guilt and shame, much of our moral upbringing is a result of our religious education or of the prevailing morality of the society in which we were raised. Additionally, as I consider myself to be a "believer" (not necessarily a follower of some specific organized religion anymore, but certainly a believer in a higher power, which I sometimes refer to as my God), I would like to take a further side trek through the realm of moral and ethical development.

The French philosopher and mystic Simone Weil (1909–1943) once noted: "We do not obtain the most precious gifts by going in search of them but by waiting for them."[30] This comes back to me now days with new force and meaning. I smile to think of my own impatience, my relative incapacity to wait for much of anything! I wonder what this is about. Why do I put so much stock in my ability to seek and find what I am looking for? Why is it so difficult for me to wait for things to unfold, to reveal themselves?

The idea that what we most deeply desire must ultimately reveal itself to us is not easy to accept. It suggests a relinquishment of control that most of us, (well me, if I am being honest), find difficult to practice. There is too much risk, too much vulnerability. Yet the willingness to relinquish control and open ourselves to the mysterious unknown is at the heart of every great spiritual tradition and the essence of most of the great mystic's message.

---

30. Simone Weil, *Waiting for God*, trans. Emma Craufurd (New York: G. P. Putnam's Sons, 1951), 112.

To say that I have been a seeker all of my life would be one of the greatest understatements ever! I have taken great pride in my ability to research and discover information. It is not just the tendency to look things up in an encyclopedia (or now days the web or Wikipedia, Google, and JSTOR). The library was my happy place. I came to love the dusty, slightly mildewy smells in the "stacks" (the name for those many floors of books in Dewey Decimal order). I could get lost for hours at a time and seemed always to walk out with more books than I had just returned. In fact, I cannot recall a time during which I did not have at least three or four books I was reading simultaneously.

However, once again I don't think I am alone in this fascinating wonderment. It is my impression that we humans were born with a hunger to seek that which is greater than ourselves. Anthropologists have found cave paintings showing that as evolution shifted the focus of our forebearers from pure hunter-gatherers to socially interdependent groupings, their creative drawings began to include thoughts of deities. The earliest of these is thought to be of a deity nicknamed "the Sorcerer" found in the caves of southern France, dating back to around the 13th century BCE. Irrespective of the question of the actual existence of God—or of a God—we humans have been asking the question for most of our history.

Beliefs, as I said, form the underpinnings of the thought-feeling-action process and are important to explore a bit more as we continue this learning to feel process. So let's take a detour through the development of a belief system. Obviously, not everyone believes in *a God* or *The God*, and it certainly is not a necessity to have a systematic theology scheme in order to have emotions or emotional responses to life. However, for those who do believe in some system that includes theological constructs as part of that sense-making, it is important to dissect how we have come to those fundamental thoughts.

Theological thoughts or systems follow the same path as moral development. Theologians James Loder[31] and James Fowler[32] have perhaps best outlined the development of religious beliefs. According to Loder, we all start with a dualistic understanding of God and life—that there is a good and a bad, a right and a wrong, and thus a God and devil behind all things. But this simple understanding cannot survive the challenges of complex life and soon breaks down into shades of rightness and wrongness. There may be ultimately God and devil poles, but in this next phase, called multiplicity, there are gradients of good and bad.

Somewhere around our teens, our moral systems move into two quick phases called "contextual relativism" and "nihilism." I clearly remember trying to justify my actions

---

31. James Loder, *The Logic of the Spirit: Human Development in Theological Perspective* (San Francisco: Jossey-Bass, 1998).

32. James Fowler, *Stages of Faith: The Psychology of Human Development and the Quest for Meaning* (New York: HarperOne, 1981).

contextually, "because the other kids were doing it!" But I must have skipped through the nihilistic phase of no rules—I seem to always have had some central gyroscope of morality. Finally, as adults, we realize that there is neither good or bad but that we must make our own decisions on what's right and wrong—for our life and for us as individuals. These mature levels of morality are called universalizing. The problem is that most people's spirituality often does not make it out of dualism or multiplicity because churches and synagogues have to teach to the lowest level of complexity, that is, dualism. And as the world becomes increasingly complex, people want to retreat to dualism for easy, pat answers.

This is truly unfortunate because as I read the teachings of the masters, most are teaching through what is called non-dual lessons. Think for example of the Zen concept of a koan—an irresolvable or unanswerable question. Spiritual development and faith only happen in the presence of doubt and situations that are unsolvable with the present level of logic. In Christianity, the best example is the so-called Beatitudes (Matthew 5). In each of the statements, Yeshua[33] presents a twist of logic (How can suffering or mourning be good or how can the poor be the richest?). And when I was finally introduced to the Gospel of Thomas[34], which alleges to be the more accurate representations of the teachings of Jesus, I saw clearly how this style was practiced by the Master. These statements, called logions, cannot be fully understood from a dualistic perspective and were most likely presented that way to confuse dualism and lead the listener toward a more advanced or complex consciousness.

Our spiritual and moral development works like that. In our dualistic first lessons, God is presented as the force of good and that which makes good things happen to good people. And, in truth, Love is like that—a force which draws us together for our common good (as the theologian Paul Tillich says[35]). But then we are confronted with priests who abuse children and our dualism cannot comprehend why a representative of this goodness would or could do such harm. Or we see an event like Newtown, Connecticut (Sandy Hook Elementary School) or more recently in Uvalde, Texas (Robb Elementary School) and cannot fathom how a God of good could allow such a thing happen to innocent children.

> Recently a coach I was supervising called me in tears of rage after learning of some early trauma in her client's history.
>
> "How the F could someone rape a four-year-old?" she screamed.
>
> "I hear your anger. How is she dealing with it?"

---

33. Yeshua of Nazareth is most likely the name of the teacher whose name was anglicized as Jesus.
34. Like the other Gospels, Thomas is estimated to have been written between 60CE and 140CE.
35. Paul Tillich, *Love, Power and Justice: Ontological Analysis and Ethical Applications* (London: Oxford University Press, 1954).

"How is *she* doing it? I don't know—I can't even deal with it. I'm so angry I am sick!"

"What is coming up for you?"

"God is supposed to watch over the little ones and 'smite' the evil ones. WTF?"

"You really feel betrayed—no wonder that hurts so much."

[tears and sobbing]

In the face of such painful realities, our belief in a "mechanical" God—what theologians call Deus ex machina, a mechanized, puppeteer God—falls away. And if we stay with our faith (that there is or must be a God), then our understanding evolves, grows, and becomes more complex. We may begin to understand that God is not a superhuman member of the League of Justice but rather the ever-present and compassionate force of love that is with us and can comfort us in our pain and grief.

In his epic novel, *Night*,[36] Elie Wiesel tells of an event when he was a child in a Nazi concentration camp. The Nazis were conducting a public hanging of some of the prisoners and among those being executed was a child. Wiesel overheard two Rabbis talking. One asked the other, "Where is our God now?" to which the second wizened Rabbi responded, pointing to the child, "Right there, suffering with us."

It takes such forces and illogical pains to rip us out of dualism because the lock dualism holds on our theological understanding also can point to any tragedy as "the work of the devil." However, that would mean if the dualism is unchecked, that the devil would be more powerful than God—yet another irresolvable concept—and how could that be? And so dualism gets blown up.

Sometimes these events can snap us forward in our development, right through multiplicity and relativism to a mature, non-dualism, or unitive consciousness. Other times they can stop us dead in our tracks. Developmental psychologists like Erik Erikson[37] and Carol Gilligan[38] teach us that the path of development is not straight and linear but moves forward and backward. There are events that can cause a developmentally mature person to fall back into dualistic thinking. For example, I was teaching a graduate class in the university once and one student, a highly accomplished HR manager at his firm, said, "Just tell me what I have to do to get an A." In a sense, he was asking, "How do I get it right?" It was a great teachable moment to point out how right and wrong are dualities that have no place in graduate school!

---

36. Elie Wiesel, *Night* (New York: Hill and Wang, 1958).

37. Erik Erikson, *Identity, Youth and Crisis* (New York: W.W. Norton & Co., 1994),

38. Carol Gilligan, *In a Different Voice: Psychological Theory and Women's Development* (Cambridge, MA: Harvard University Press, 2009).

One day in my morning prayer and contemplation time I actually fell into a conversation with this in-welling divine voice.

"Look, I have tried all my life to tell you that I'm not fit to be a minister, and you keep showing up in my thoughts and as my inner voice. I give up. I am surrendering to you and what you want me to do. So, what is it? Tell me, what do you want me to do?"

"If I told you, you would try to do it your way. Are you really surrendering?"

"Yes—I give up. You're in charge."

"Good. Then trust and take that leap of faith."

"Wait, you aren't going to tell me what you want from me?"

"No—you do not get to know. Trust and take the next step forward."

In remembering this conversation, I noticed that I was still coming from right/wrong duality in expecting the divine voice to tell me what was the right thing to do. But what resulted from this exchange was that at each decision point, the start of each day or in examining my day before going to sleep, I check my feeling and experience. Had I done what was intended for me, or in facing a new day, what is it that I should do today that would be aligned with my purpose? Where is that leap of faith today?

From the perspective of my own life, I followed a similar path to that which the Loder and Fowler models describe. Like all kids in my hometown, I had my fair share of Sunday school religious training. And as a child constantly curious about this "God" thing, it fit the bill. But as Loder says, it worked only so long. My questioning pushed the complexity factor and my reading fueled a deeper understanding. But that was about as far as the organized church could take me.

While the church and organized religion carry with them some (perhaps many) distortions of what the great teachers and sacred texts have said, there still remains in each of us a desire for connection. Perhaps this might explain why some people still stay affiliated with their church even after these atrocities and events have dislodged them from their dualism. But it is this connection—with each other and with the *one* of everything—that is at the core of spirituality. What I have found, and what I believe all spiritual paths point to as the fundamental drive in humans, is that we all have the desire to love and to be loved – and I will get further into that in the next chapter.

It is unfortunate that so many groups pervert that desire to be loved and to love into a limited small set of "us" and build exclusionary walls to keep others out. Irrespective of that, the core of spirituality is and always has been a journey toward oneness—toward total inclusion. The great teachers of the world all teach that love is the way and that love is the answer. Why else would that be such a strong and common theme except that it is a call to tear down the barriers between us and them, between each other? Love can dissolve those barriers if and when we let it.

Our human need for acceptance and belonging is actually a need for love.[39] Studies show that orphaned infants who do not receive enough touch and loving affection fail to thrive and often even die. It is that essential a need. So why is it that we so often attempt to create belonging by creating bonds around vilification of the other —the ones not in our special group?

Most of you are probably familiar with the classic novel *Lord of the Flies* by William Golding. *Lord of the Flies* is fiction (we presume) but around the same time—in fact a year before the publication of *Lord of the Flies*—a team of social psychologists led by Muzafer Sherif conducted an experiment with a group of twenty-two boys at a summer camp at Robber's Cave State Park. The infamous "Robber's Cave Experiment" set out to establish the formation of group adhesion and in-group versus out-group attitudes, including what happens when they are in competition and in conflict for scarce resources or when they are compelled to work together toward a common goal unachievable by either group independently.[40]

What Sherif and his colleagues found was that when people feel that they are competing for limited or scarce resources like food and water they rapidly came together more strongly, but did so by competing with and vilifying the other group. The boys' behaviors included name-calling, burning the other team's flag, raiding their cabin and stealing from each other—even if what they were competing for were simply prizes or recognition. This finally broke into outright violence which had to be broken up by the counselors (researchers who were acting as the counselors). Sharif and his team coined the term for this process: "out-grouping."

Apparently however, the fighting scared the researchers sufficiently that they felt the need to change directions. The experimenters quickly shifted to attempts to build unity and reconciliation by setting up a mutual need and, to their amazement, the boys almost immediately started working together to solve their mutual problem. But the lessons from the Robber's Cave Experiment were impressive (and are partly pardoned because the study was conducted prior to the field of psychology establishing rules around the treatment of human subjects). One lesson is that we tend to bond even with strangers by finding a common enemy. We see that even today as our political leaders attempt to unite parties and even the nation by finding some other group, political party or outside force they can scapegoat as the common enemy. But the bigger lesson is that we will come together out

---

39. Carol Gilligan, *The Birth of Pleasure: A New Map of Love* (New York: Vintage/Random House, 2002).

40. Carolyn Sherif was my undergrad professor of social psychology classes at Penn State (circa 1970) and brought her husband, Muzafer in as a guest lecturer on several occasions, though there are also many articles available on the study.

of mutual concern to solve a problem even when coming together means working with others we had thought were the "bad guys." I am placing my faith in the latter lesson that we can overcome our differences and band together to solve the crises of hunger, climate change, and divisiveness.

Through all this interpretation of the world as good or bad and for me or against me, we continue the search to love and be loved. We may not directly say "I love my buddies or besties"—as that might feel weird—but it is, in essence, a sense of being loved and belonging. My best friend may have done something wrong or perhaps didn't show up for me, but that is excused by the overarching unconditionality we hold for our beloved best friend. They can do no wrong in our eyes.

What breaks us free from the earlier stages of moral development is when we experience a person who we had judged or categorized as wrong or bad does something good, or, in the reverse, when someone who we have previously thought was good and infallible does something wrong or unethical.

> In 2001 I went with my men's team to Nepal to hike the Annapurna Sanctuary. We landed and stayed in Kathmandu for three days. Kathmandu was the most polluted city I had ever experienced and as a contact lens wearer, it was horrible. On the fourth day we set out for the starting point, Pokhara, and my itchy eyes got worse and worse. By the time we reached Pokhara, the infection was so great that my eyes were almost swollen shut. The doctor at the local hospital said that I could not go "back country" until I was better, lest I go blind.
>
> I came out and told my team that they had to go on without me, and one man, my good friend Mike, immediately said, "You're not staying alone. I will stay with you." Now Mike might not always show up when he says he will, and sometimes he is not true to his word. But because of that one incident, I will forever excuse any grievance or action that others might write him off for. He did not leave me behind and I will never forget that one act.

In our quest to be loved and belong to someone or some group, we subjugate our sense of right and wrong to the greater need of being loved (remember, by the time we reach adulthood, we have come to the conclusion that there is no right or wrong except by our own definition). This is what we bring into our courtship and romantic adventures and is probably what is behind falling blindly in love! We learn to excuse these errors and omissions on the part of our lover or loved ones, because we have fully accepted them as "good." However, after the initial honeymoon phases of the relationship are over, those same "excused" behaviors may become problematic for us and may erode the foundation of love in the relationship.

Questions to ponder:

1. Where are you on your development path?

2. What were the events and catalysts that moved you from fundamental dualism to the later stages of multiplicity, relativism, and mature choice?

3. How did you feel when you first discovered that there really is no right or wrong?

9

To Love and Be Loved

So what does all of this have to do with love and being loved? Somewhere, situated between the need for belonging and the sense of some higher power, is the need for love. Almost all of us have experienced a feeling of love. It was welded in place at the first moment we emerged from our mother's womb. That first gaze between the mother and the newborn infant is a gaze of pure love. We looked into those eyes for the first time with absolute trust (actually we had no other choice). Here looking back at us was the source from whence we came, whose heartbeat signature we already knew, who would hold us to her breast and provide sustenance. She was our world, our everything! And that unnamed experience was our first taste of love.

Though things rapidly changed, we never forget that first experience of love, and its lingering aftertaste is something we would search for the rest of our lives. Love is perhaps the purest of emotions along with perhaps peace and joy. But love has such power and touches something so deeply within us that it feels almost supernatural. Perhaps some of us feel that sensation a bit in our family of origin—but that itself is fraught with other conflicting and competing dynamics. And some families are so busy, twisted up or just plain too big for us to really experience that singular feeling we first felt in bonding with mom.

We then turn outward on our quest to be loved. We think we feel it again when our eyes meet our first person of interest. There it is again, at first as just a flutter inside, but it has some element of recognizable familiarity. We also feel a twinge of being loved in our band of brothers or sisters—our "besties." Placed in a new and unfamiliar setting like the boys in the Robber's Cave camp, we want that sense of unconditional acceptance, and we will do all sorts of things just to get that. We will even shun others so that the ones we call "we" and "us" will feel closer together. My small band of boys was only four or five of us, but we have stayed in communication to this day, despite having lost a couple as we have grown older.

As we grow and mature into our teens, the litmus test of relationships is our sense of being loved or of loving some other being. However, that now gets some high-octane fuel in the form of our emerging sex hormones. Those gazes of first love or infatuation stir up something extra inside! But it is still the quest to be loved and to love. And if we are among the fortunate, we fall "in love" for the first time—some forever and some for the first of many such experiences. Being "in love" is a state wherein we feel as if we are again floating in a pool of unconditional love and acceptance. That is the second experience welded in place.

"Love is not something we give or get," says Brené Brown, "it is something we nurture and grow, a connection that can be cultivated between two people only when it exists within each one of them—we can love others only as much as we love ourselves."[41] Essentially it is that seed, planted by our mother's gaze, that we must nurture and grow. But importantly, as Brown contends, we must first learn how to love ourselves—to turn that feeling from a single source into something we can do for ourselves. When, and if, we have that foundation of love from birth through our younger years, it provides not only the model for our self-love but allows us to know how we get to feel *about* ourselves.

I thoroughly believe that the need to be loved and to give love is as fundamental a need as our need to find food and shelter. The need for love is something that we all share to some degree. Of course, we all know those fiercely independent folks who claim that they do not have a *need* for love, but I still have seen them love others deeply and allow themselves to be loved unconditionally, irrespective of their calling it a need or not.

Research has shown time and time again that being in a loving relationship is a primary determinant of happiness and satisfaction in life. Most of us are familiar with Abraham Maslow's hierarchy of needs, where the need for love and belonging ranks third after physiological and safety needs. But I would argue that love is at least as important and perhaps the most foundational of the needs. Newborn babies that are not held and cuddled experience a failure to thrive and can often die as a result. And I wish I could find the study I once read which demonstrated that just holding hands lowered a person's blood pressure and stress. Being touched or holding hands is shown to lower cortisol (associated with stress) and increase the production of oxytocin (often referred to as the love hormone), both of which will decrease stress. For me, touch is my primary love language (see Gary

---

41. Brown, *Atlas*, 187.

Chapman's book on love languages),[42] so my craving touch—holding hands, a stroke of my hair, whatever—in my relationship is how I experience love and acceptance.

The need for love is not a weakness or something we should be ashamed to admit. It is a healthy and essential part of being human. When we embrace our need for love, it frees us to be receptive to all these wonderful benefits. So perhaps instead of calling it a need, we should just refer to is as a core element of the human condition and of the persons we choose to love. I love this quote from Rumi: "Your task is not to seek for love, but merely to seek and find all the barriers within yourself that you have built against it." Really!

Combining what Rumi is saying with an understanding of the need to love and be loved, I can actually feel the tension of that wrestling match. Our need to be loved is so fundamental, yet we do so much to protect ourselves from its power. Why is that? Why would we work so hard to build those barriers if it is the most fundamental of needs? As I feel around inside my own being for the answer, I sense that it is a result of my feeling so vulnerable in the act of loving.

It might make things a bit clearer if I separate romantic love from the basic need to be loved. Much has been written about romantic love and its evolution over time as we mature. Romantic love starts with an infatuation with the loved one and with a narcissistic need to be important to someone else (OMG I remember my first crush—I could not stop thinking about her). Infatuation also triggers a chemical reaction (i.e., we feel the chemistry) between one person and another. Perhaps it is our reaction to pheromones or the attraction to the scent of the other. For me I can remember that every time my first girlfriend and I touched or kissed there was an actual spark between us. It was as if we were two electrical beings that discharged with touch. But whatever the source was, we just cannot get the obsession with our loved one out of our minds. And along with that obsession is a parallel form of narcissistic self-love which is the hope that we are loved, fawned over, and obsessed about in the same way ("Oh, wouldn't that be nice," we think.).

After infatuation, if and when we create a relationship with our loved one, we move into a more "comfortable" attraction. Here, we are not as supercharged on sexual hormones but have found even our lover's idiosyncrasies attractive. This is the type of love that the theologian James Loder describes as the "non-possessive delight in the particularities of another." Yeah, that! We simply adore and delight in their presence in our lives. But moreover, it is the "delighting in the particularities" that resonates so well with me. We love not so much for our many similarities but from our loved one's unique characteristics, which we find to be sweet and endearing.

And from there we can flow into several levels of deepening emotional bonds. As we continue in an intentional loving relationship, we find more and better ways to express

---

42. Gary Chapman, *The 5 Love Languages: the Secret to Love that Lasts*, 5th ed. (Chicago: Northfield Publishing, 2015).

our love. I qualify these relationships as intentional, because there are many mature relationships that fall into a lackluster level of living together that simply takes the other's presence as a granted, foregone conclusion; and I am not referring to those. For us to mature and deepen the loving emotional connection we must actively work on it. It's not laborious work, but is what I call "being intentional" about loving and being loved.

I have always delighted in this scene in Fiddler on the Roof:

> "Do you love me?" Tevye asks Golde, his wife of twenty-five years.
>
> Her response is nonplussed, "Do I love you? What kind of question is that with our daughters getting married. And this trouble in the town. You're upset, you're worn out. Go inside, go lie down! Maybe it's indigestion."
>
> "Golde, I'm asking you a question, do you love me?"
>
> "You're a fool," she answers. "I know," Tevye says, "But do you love me."
>
> … (after a short exchange, Golde answers)
>
> "I'm your wife."
>
> "I know, but… do you love me."
>
> Golde turns to the audience and sings, "Do I love him?
> For twenty-five years I've lived with him,
> Fought him, starved with him.
> Twenty-five years my bed is his,
> If that's not love, what is?
>
> "Then you do love me?" Tevye asks again.
>
> "I suppose I do," Golde answers, finally. "And I suppose I love you, too," says Tevye, smiling contentedly.

Perhaps that is an example of mature love mixed with that habituated, taken-for-granted type of mature love, but those bonding experiences shared by Tevye and Golde, were the places where an arranged marriage turned into a deepening love for each other. Or perhaps our learning to love someone is like my friend Sam Keen said, "We come to love not by finding a perfect person, but by learning to see an imperfect person perfectly."[43]

Aside from romantic and erotic love, there is also what Plato classified as *philia*, "brotherly love." And that might be more of what Loder was describing in his definition of delighting in the unique particularities of another. To be loved in that way might be categorized as

---

43. Sam Keen, *To Love and Be Loved* (New York: Bantam Books, 1999).

a sense of unconditional love. It is the kind of pure love that we first experienced in our mother's gaze, what we nurtured and turned into an unconditional love of self, and which we need and want in our lives from others.

But what of the need *to* love—to love others or another. I get why we need and want to be loved, but what causes us to want to give that to others? Is it simply the maturation of our first desires to be loved which turns into giving that back to the one who loves us? It appears that this too is hardwired to our own pleasure and comfort. We want to love and care for others as part of our evolution. As one of the more fragile and vulnerable of the species, we needed to deeply care for our young for a longer period of time than other mammals. A foal or calf stands and walks almost immediately on birth, but it takes a human infant nearly a year to do that, even shakily. Loving and nurturing our young is a built-in necessity.

From a purely physiological standpoint, loving releases several chemicals in our brain that increase the likelihood of our doing it again and again. In fact, each different type and stage of love releases differing chemicals. For example, simply being attracted to another human releases serotonin and dopamine, while lust releases either testosterone or estrogen, and attachment produces higher levels of oxytocin. These hormones, drugs or chemicals—depending on how you want to classify them—have the effect of having us want more of them. You could almost say that love has some addictive properties, but I won't go that far!

I hesitate to get into Darwin's theories of love's role in evolution, but I cannot resist the temptation! Briefly, while he believed that love was a higher function of evolution and one that separated mammals from, say, reptiles, he also had a certain disdain for love itself. And though he eventually did marry (actually his first cousin, Emma), he conceded that it was because "one cannot live this solitary life, with groggy old age, friendless, cold and childless, staring one in one's face already beginning to wrinkle." So, in deciding whether to marry Emma, Darwin made a pair of lists: "Marry" and "Not Marry." Under the list of "Not Marry" were things like "freedom to travel" and "being able to read in the evenings." Under "Marry" he listed things like "charms," "music," "female chitchat," and "better than a dog, anyhow!"

Perhaps Darwin should have known better than to marry his own first cousin since he had conducted research on in-breeding in animals and noticed that plants fared far better when exposed to a diversity of pollinators and species. It seems like his marriage to Emma was more of a convenience and falling into line with the expectations of his society than out of any love or lust for Emma.

Nonetheless, among his later scholarly writings was *The Expressions of the Emotions in Man and Animals* where he did dig into the feelings of love. In that text, Darwin frequently used the word love to describe certain mating behaviors. But many scholars think it was a word he preferred over sex, given the morality of the times.

The one takeaway from Darwin is that he was the first to postulate that emotions came from the second level of our brains, the limbic brain or the cerebellum. Reptiles, which have only the most primitive part of the brain (the medulla), would actually eat their young, whereas animals with more advanced brains cared for both their young and others of their species.

Now, back to the question of our "need" to love. Is it a need or an evolutionary mechanism for the preservation of the species? Is it the product of our hormones or the addiction to the hormones produced by loving and being loved? Whatever the case, it would appear that we humans do in fact have some sort of need to love each other, and, by extension, to get involved in relationships that deepen and strengthen those loving urges over time.

That was certainly true for me. While my mom was somewhat affectionate, she later told me, in one of our many conversations as she aged into her eighties and nineties, that she thought she was a terrible mother and that she never liked being a mother. It had ruined her figure, she said, and detracted from her ability to be with her love (my dad). This was in stark contrast to the observation that everyone referred to her as "mom." People would come to where she worked as a receptionist or a bank teller, just to talk with her. She was that kind of caring and compassionate listener.

Dad on the other hand was a stoic. My brother and I really think that the war stole all of his emotions and his soul from him. We know that he had to have killed during the war and that must have stolen his soul, as it does for many soldiers. He never talked about the war except to say that he "did his job." But what I learned from others was that he was quite a hero.

Dad graduated in 1942, but the day after Pearl Harbor he and his classmates all enlisted in the army and shipped out right after graduation. What I learned about him as a soldier came from my girlfriends' fathers (his classmates) on more than several occasions. I would go to pick up my date on a Friday or Saturday evening, and her dad would meet me at the door. "Are you Bill Girrell's son?" he would say, rather sternly. "Yessir." "Well Bill saved my life, so I imagine you are okay. Be safe and have her home on time." "Yessir," I'd reply rather humbly. Dad never told us why, but he had earned a Bronze Star for valor in battle on several occasions. Later in life, when the Internet provided the tools, I finally found out what he did from the brief description in the military chronicles and an article in the archives of our hometown paper.

The curious thing about my father was that he was not only a decorated war hero, he was a major in the army at the time of his death, though he had held the ranks of private to first lieutenant three times during the war. Apparently, he didn't like following orders that much! We knew he was a leader, to be sure. But the curious thing was that his civilian job was that of a bottle washer at a brewery. Not the foreman, not the union steward, just a plain worker bee. My brother and I could never figure out why someone who was clearly a leader never was a leader outside of the military. That is until one day it dawned on us that he wasn't a leader; he was a warrior. And what does a warrior do when there is no war? It doesn't matter. He was just waiting for the next war. Unfortunately he died before he could ever serve in Vietnam.

But all of that led to making him a stoic. He rarely expressed any emotion, and I don't think I ever heard him say "I love you" to any of the three of us kids. So deep inside of me there was a longing to be loved—if not by my father, then by someone. I didn't want someone to "suppose" that they loved me, like Golde; I needed to be loved for who I was, just as I was. Like Tevye, I wanted to know.

Questions to Ponder:

1. What was it like when you first felt loved by someone outside your family?

2. How has logic, religion, education, family, and your social upbringing shaped your ability to feel and even defining what you believe is right and wrong?

3. How and where does self-worth and the need to be loved play into your way of being and your ways of acting?

Part Three:

Welcome to the Jungle

10

The Inner Journey of the "Hero's Quest"

What are the things that teach us to feel, not just to know about feelings and emotions, but what are those things that cause us to experience the feeling and teach us what it means?

Fathers always want to teach their sons humility to prepare them for the cruel, nasty world "out there." At least my dad did, and this fell under the guise of teaching me a life lesson. One day, my father took a bucket and ran the water hose in it until it was about three-fourths full.

> "Put your fist into the water," he instructed. "Now pull it out really fast and see how big a hole you left."

Of course the water closed in where my hand was, not leaving a trace of my fist's presence.

> "That's how much you will be remembered after you die. The world won't even notice."

Without hesitation, I took the garden hose and filled the bucket to the very top. Then, I once again plunged my fist into the bucket, this time displacing the full volume of my hand. When I pulled it out, the water level had dropped a corresponding amount. "I will make a difference," I said with all the defiance of a normal teenager.

> "Smart ass!" was all the praise I got for not acknowledging his life lesson.

The classic quest, whether it is the Hero's Quest or simply the quest of self-discovery, eventually becomes an inner quest. For many the ultimate symbol of this self-discovery takes the form of The Hero's Quest. But modern-day mythology has the Hero story all wrong. Today we celebrate the superheroes with their superpowers that surmount any obstacle and defeat any opponent. The Marvel hero always triumphs. The result, however, is a false belief that we should and can overcome any obstacle, any challenge, and emerge the hero! "You can be anything you put your mind to," says the modern myth.

But that is not the essence of the meta-myth of The Hero's Quest. In its classic form, the hero, who is off on a quest to find meaning and self-understanding, is mortally wounded and finds his soul (or hers) *through* the wound. The hero finally understands that we are not immortal and will eventually die. Stripped of their false sense of immortality, the hero learns the lesson they set out to discover: It is not what you do that makes for greatness; it is who you are. It is how you handle adversity and is a way of being that encounters the world with full acceptance for what it is. In the end, the hero had nothing to prove, no grail to discover, no golden fleece to bring home. Rather, the hero has to come to accept life on life's terms.

Modern medicine looks upon death as a mistake, a failure. It views its job as that of preserving life at all costs and in doing so often denies people of the dignity of a normal death. They (doctors) seem to believe that death is a separate element apart from life instead of embracing the reality that birth, life, and death are all part of one journey. That makes it even more difficult for the modern hero to learn that same vital lesson that the legendary hero Percival, one of King Arthur's Knights of the Round Table, had to learn.

The hero must bend to the forces of nature and life and not the other way around. Anyone who has ever climbed a serious mountain will tell you that. They start off with high ambition: "I will conquer this mountain." But the pitches get steeper and the rocks offer fewer handholds. And while some spots afford a great vista, the struggle of the continual climb is humbling. Often there are what we refer to as "false summits." You are certain that you are nearing the peak because you can see sky ahead, only to find out that it is just a momentary leveling off before the next upward pitch.

The air gets thinner somewhere around 10-12,000 feet, and you have to stop every 20 or 30 steps to suck in more oxygen. Your fingertips begin to tingle. And still no summit is in sight. Long ago you passed through the cloud layer so you no longer have those beautiful views of the valley below. Now it is just you and the mountain, like an island floating in a sea of clouds. If you stick with it, you do eventually reach the peak, but it is not in victory. The feeling is one of gratitude: Nature has allowed you to survive and has quietly, gracefully welcomed you, in your humility, to her secret place. I remember the first time I summited a high peak: I knelt in prayer and honored the mountain who had let me in on her secret. It was a sacred moment—not a victory. You may have taken pictures of these places before, but they do not convey the feeling, show the steep pitch of the trail, and, even if they did, your friends would not understand the feeling at the top. Heroes are humbled and humble. But the mountain is just a metaphor for the real deal of the inner quest.

Most of us start our quest into adulthood by trying to find a real career, knowing that wasn't the answer, but that it was going to be a way to pay for quest. At least, that was my experience. In college I had studied psychology and counseling and in my internship as a master's candidate, I found that I was good at career counseling and decided to give that a go. But higher education paid pitifully low salaries. So I eventually left to find greener pastures.

It is said that the darkest hour is just before the dawn and for me that seemed to be the case. Life had been beating me down, it seemed, and after two divorces and an unrewarding career, I had gotten nowhere on my quest—in fact, I felt like I was a failure. One dark night, sitting alone in my office, I contemplated ending it all. But something inside me said there is more to life than this. I needed to find a firmer foundation. So I started by taking every self-improvement course I could find. Some had great potential, but the half-life of weekend programs is about two weeks, in my experience, meaning that every two weeks the power and impact reduced by about 50% of what it had been before. I needed to do the inner work myself and not look for some outside program or workshop to do it for me.

Personal transformation programs had become popular in the late eighties and were built on several principles. First and foremost was that they were based in adult education theory. As children, our minds are a blank slate, and the teacher can write new information, as it were, on that slate for us to learn. But as adults, we have found that our experience is better than anything a teacher could tell us. In researching adult learning, psychologists at places like the National Training Labs and Silva Mind Control had found that the educator must first respect the fact that the person possessed knowledge to begin with. But then, in order to learn something new or different, the adult would have to unlearn that old information before the new idea could move in. At first, these programs used what was called Marathon Encounters—a three-day session that continued without stop (read that as without sleep) until the participants' resistance was low enough to break through their barriers.

Subsequently, researchers found that those old ideas did not go quietly into the night. If they went at all, they would have to go kicking and screaming. In other words, these new learning systems had to present intense situations over a sustained period of time, such that the person's defenses were lowered and the old ideals could be blown up. The Marathon Encounter was replaced with something more powerfully intense. Enter the world of Werner Erhardt and EST, along with its offsprings: Landmark Worldwide, Insight

Seminars, and Lifespring. While often labeled as cults, because of the focused power of their trainers, these programs were power-packed and indeed transformative. They had it all: long hours, powerful trainers who understood the source of thoughts and emotions, and exercises that were high speed and high intensity.

But personal transformation was not a one-and-done event. Rather, it had to be practiced over time, which meant that the student enrolled in ever greater and more powerful sessions that practiced and honed the skills learned in the basic event. And practice it, I did—Lifespring style.[44]

In most of these programs there is a place where, after having broken down the old and less functional ways of being, the student was asked questions about their dreams and desires. But this was no casual conversation—it was a full-out Rotor-Rooter technique. I was sitting in a chair with a fellow student on either side and was bombarded with rapid-fire questions, screamed at me for an insanely long period of time. My job, as the one in the "hot seat" was to answer as fast as possible, without thinking. The purpose was to get to the unconscious desire without the censorship of one's conscious mind. Things come out that the student didn't realize were even there. And in the middle of it all, out of my mouth came the words, "I want to be a minister. I want to do what God created me for."

Wait, what? I had all but forgotten my calling, but there it was, rising from the depths of my subconscious. So what do I do with that? I had found a career in the corporate outplacement arena. I had found and would eventually marry to the woman of my dreams, but this core desire had still been untouched. Again, I felt a sense of guilt—not over what I had done this time, but rather over what I had not done.

Thirty-five years after first entering seminary as a naïve kid of twenty-two, I walked back into the same seminary. "It's a long story," I began to explain to the admissions officer. "Look around," she smiled, "You aren't alone." Thirty-five years earlier seminaries were populated with young men like myself and very, very few women. But now that had been replaced by second- and third-career people, the majority of whom were women. Seminaries had changed. Theology had changed. And I had changed enough to reenter.

Since I was employed at this point as a leadership coach for the firm, I told them I wanted to learn more about leadership. My field of psychology had perhaps 50 or 60 years of research on the topic of leadership, but theology had literally thousands of years of information and stories about great leaders. And not just in the Judeo-Christian world; leadership was the topic of the *Tao Te Ching* and *I Ching*, of Confucius's writing, and of Master Sun Tzu. I wanted to see what concepts I could port over and secularize for our work with leaders.

---

44. As a participant, I committed not to reveal the nature or content of any of these exercises and, some thirty years later, I wish to still honor that commitment, so the questions shall remain a mystery for you. Suffice it to say that it worked for me.

The very first course I took was called The Soul of the Leader. In it, the professor (who was also the author of the text[45]) described something called the "dark night of the soul." It is a place where all of that in which you believed—that was the basis for explaining and understanding the way the world is—no longer explains your current reality. This was also true for the leader, where all of the theories from B-school couldn't rally the troops in crisis, and the leader had to unlearn and relearn a new set of core beliefs and actions. I immediately recognized is as the story of my own spiritual journey

The concept of the dark night came from a 16th century Spanish mystic named John of the Cross (Juan de la Cruz, and it described what happened spiritually as those old simplistic levels of understanding no longer fit your complex world. I was captivated! It was the story of my spiritual journey. Juan had been ordained but really wanted to be in residence at a certain monastery. However when he talked about the visions he was having, those very priests whom he so admired tried him as a heretic and threw him in the dungeon.[46] The cell was very small and had only one small window high up on the side. Juan was essentially starved and was only brought out once a day to be flogged while the other monks were having their meal. How was it possible for men of God to inflict such violence?

Suffering from malnutrition and the infections of his wounds, Juan found his spirit became even stronger. He made up and memorized a poem (he had no paper or pen) which he called "The Dark Night of the Soul." (n.d.) After nine months of this torture and close to death, one night Juan escaped and was rescued by a group of nuns who brought him to their convent where they nursed him back to life. During his recovery, however, he would recite some of the poem, which the nuns found fascinating but didn't understand. His book by the same name[47] is his explanation of the poem and stands as one of the best descriptions of the elements of the dark night passage. We will dig into exactly what happens in the dark night a bit more in the next chapter.

Whether on a spiritual quest or a personal inward journey, the end goal of such a quest is to become one with reality. On the hero's quest, the journeyman learns through sometimes multiple "dark night" experiences that life is in charge. Any pretense of being in control of his fate gets taken away by the harsh reality of the journey. The hero learns finally that it is not about winning the game. There is no score to be kept. It is not about winning at all—it is learning how to open up to receive the lessons of life. Rilke's poem "The Man

---

45. Margaret Benefiel, *The Soul of a Leader: Finding Your Path to Success and Fulfillment* (New York: Crossroad Publishing, 2008).

46. What may have happened in reality was that the Inquisitors learned of Juan's heritage. His father was Jewish "converso" and his mother an Islamic Moor. So in the name of "purity" and as a disguise for their racial bigotry, the charges of heresy were perhaps trumped up in order to remove this embarrassing man.

47. St. John of the Cross, *Dark Night of the Soul*, trans. Mirabai Starr (New York: Riverhead, 2002). While several translations of this text, most notably by Alison Peers, exist, I find Starr's translation to be more poetic and probably in sync with John's intention.

Watching" ends with the couplet, "This is how he grows, by being defeated decisively by constantly greater beings."[48]

All of these different paths—the hero's journey, personal transformation courses, the dark night of the soul— are describing the same process. In order for us to regain our innocence and be able to see the world as it is, we need to be stripped of our arrogant self-centeredness. It is the message of every sage,[49] or every major religion and of all these different journeys. The hero's journey is a decent into death or near-death, going to "hell and back" in order to become opened once again to the mysteries of living. It is a rich experience despite being fraught with pain and frustration. And it is certainly one worth describing in a bit more detail.

> **Questions to ponder:**
>
> 1. Where have you been humbled or brought to your knees by forces outside of yourself?
>
> 2. What were your lessons learned on the path?
>
> 3. If you've gone on a vision quest or spiritual quest, what were your insights?

---

48. Robert Bly, *Selected Poems of Rainer Maria Rilke*, trans. and ed. Robert Bly (New York: Harper & Row, 1981).

49. Throughout this text I will refer generically to the "sages" of humankind. What I am specifically referring to are people who have shaped and guided our collective societies by their teaching and writing. They include (but are by no means limited to) Lao Tzu, Confucius, the unknown authors of the Upanishads and Vedas, Solomon, David, Hillel the elder, Aristotle and Plato, Jesus of Nazareth, Paul, Hafiz, Rumi, Aquinas, and the list goes on. Essentially, I have found that if something lands as a truth, it is true for all, and therefore we find those truths appearing in all of these sages' teachings.

11

Impasse, Failure, and Transformation

"I'm leaving you," she said rather matter-of-factly over morning coffee.

"What are you talking about?"

"I mean, I don't want to be married to you anymore."

"Can we talk about this? You seem . . ."

"No. I've made up my mind and I'm moving out on Saturday. Besides I have fallen in love with someone else."

That was a showstopper. End of conversation. Beginning of my first dark night experience. My wife of only two and a half years had already decided that we were history.

How do we deal with such events that feel so devastating? Certainly not all of the events that force our growth and transformation are devastating. Some are felt as impasses, hurdles so big or daunting that they seem almost impossible to surmount. Some of them are failures that we have brought on ourselves, that cannot be "blamed" on someone else or some outside forces. But whatever the case, failures, impasses and hard knocks not only set us down, they can cause us to radically shift how we act and how we perceive the world around us.

Picking up on the story of Juan de la Cruz let's take a look at how he described the dark night passage. Because of how John wrote about the dark night passage, many people think of it as a linear process (first this, then that). But the truth of the dark night is that it simply has four major recognizable elements which happen in no particular sequence. Think of this like a sort of two-by-two box. One of the dynamics of the dark night is that there are active elements, things that the seeker—the person on the quest—does to further the quest, and passive elements, things that percolate in the subconscious mind and develop without out intentional interventions.

The other side of the two-by-two box are the two separate realms of the senses and the spirit. The realm of senses is comprised of, as you may guess, your ability to perceive and understand through the five senses. On the spiritual side, Juan said that our understanding about God, nature and the universe exist of a sense of wonder combined with one's sense of "understanding" what those things are.

In other words there are times when the seeker is actively using their senses to perceive what is going on and there are times when those feelings seem to arise out of nowhere. Likewise, there are times when the seeker is aware of, and actively seeking to understand their place in the universe and their sense of the divine. There are also times when either that feels like a stupid thought or when a sudden sense of being loved and cradled by Universe or Mother Earth (whatever) just wells up from inside for no apparent reason.

We all have a need for sense-making. It's the primary job of our brains. While we are continually sifting through gazillions of stimuli, experiencing the experience and having reactions—emotional reactions—to those experiences, our brains are speedily processing, categorizing, sorting, and naming those data—all in the name of making sense of it.

For the most part this sense-making results in meta-structures—belief systems—that then form a basis for further sense-making in the future. And typically things that don't make sense or don't fit into the template are either filed away as exceptions or outright dismissed.

But every once in a while, an event happens that is so profound, so overwhelming and powerful that it shakes us at the very foundation of our sense-making. Said another way, our beliefs no longer can explain or make sense out of what just happened. At that point, we can either go into denial about the current events or we must let go of the beliefs and evolve them to a new and different level—one that might help us process and understand the new world of our experiences.

In the spiritual world these experiences are called "the dark night of the soul"—so called because, in the space between the old belief system and finding the next iteration of beliefs, there is a place of nothingness, like being in a dark room without any light. An example might be that you had a belief that God is good and does good things to good people and bad things to bad people. That's fine when we are children, but at some point, the world throws us a monkey wrench that doesn't fit the paradigm—like Sandy Hook Elementary School and Uvalde, Texas massacres mentioned before. We are no longer able to hold on to those more fundamental beliefs. That is what Wiesel was referring to, where the one Rabbi couldn't handle what was happening within his original religious beliefs.

But the dark night is not confined to the spiritual realm. On one level, such experiences cause our development, and on a deeper lever they can also strip away our egoistic belief that we have some control and understanding of the world around us. These experiences throw us into a kind of nowhere-land of nothingness. Suddenly nothing makes sense. Everything falls apart. Religion and beliefs feel stupid and senseless. And for many people, that nothingness hangs around for an insufferably long time. That is the dark night of the soul.

The dark night is a transformational passage in the fullest sense of the word. Formation is the process of creating our self-identity, but when that falls apart as a result of one of these profoundly shaking experiences, we must reform our identity. In truth, it is a process of moving from formation through transformation into re-formation.

We refer to it as the dark night because, as I said, it often feels as scary as being alone in a dark room at night time. In some of the early experiments in the field of psychology, participants were placed in a totally darkened room with absolutely no ambient light. There was, however, one pinpoint of light that came from a small hole on one wall. And, despite the fact that the light source was fixed and immovable, the people in the room reported that it moved all over the place–so much and so fast that they actually reported getting nauseous. In total darkness with no other referent points, any information (or in this case, a point of light) will make no sense and will confuse us. It's that way in the dark night of the soul as well. With our former sense-making structure dashed to pieces, there is no referent point and nothing makes sense.

Nothing, that is, until we reform our new and evolved belief structure. That process is often subconscious. We may not be aware of what is happening—only that we feel confused, upset, out-of-sorts and totally disconnected from everyone and everything.

That is what happened when my first wife announced that she was leaving. I was at that point still a naïve young backwoods boy with a set of storybook fantasies about how life and marriage should work. No one I knew ever got divorced. Couples either worked it out or they suffered through it and then buried it away. But I had no model for how to deal with her announcement, and I had no frame of reference for how to work on relationship problems, infidelity or whatever.

We were just young lovers and products of the "love generation." Both of us had multiple sexual experiences and both of us had fallen in and out of love before, but this was different. It was absolute. Done deal. And it felt like a door had been slammed shut in my face. I felt like there was no recourse and was left alone trying to make sense out of a totally unpredictable event for which my belief structures had no antecedent preparation. So when I am asked how I felt about it, I am perplexed, because it was beyond the realm of feelings and smack-dab in the darkness and nothingness of a dark night experience.

Let me pause for a moment to point out that there is a huge difference between transformation and change. In general, change is what happens when some outside system is altered and we must adapt to it. Say, for example, your company is bought out by another firm and you suddenly have a new boss and new set of expectations and work requirements. Nothing really changes inside of you. You simply must change your patterns and habits a bit to adapt to the new normal.

Transformation, on the other hand, is a radical upheaval of your inner gyroscope and belief system. How you thought of yourself in relation to the outside world or some other person(s) has to be rewired. And while that sounds like it's just another form of change, it is profoundly different. We may have a few problems coping with the new boss or work expectations, but we eventually cope and move on. But with transformation, we are knocked on our asses and don't know how to cope or often even what it would mean to "cope" with this upheaval. And the amount of time it takes for this transformation to happen and rewire us is totally unpredictable. Sometimes a dark night experience is just a day-long event, but some can last for months or years. What appears to be the determinant of the length of time it takes for the transformation to take root is how attached we are to our old views and values.

And it is transformation that causes us to grow and develop. Often adapting to changes does not require much of us. It falls within the realm of the normal or new normal. Developmental transformation is an entirely different realm. To be clear, not everyone is transformed from a dark night experience. Some people retreat into their old ways. Some fall back to dualism.

It is only when we are confronted by these irresolvable conflicts that the old logic (stage of moral and ethical development) must give way to the next level. It is how we develop. We can think of the dark night as one huge irresolvable dilemma that either forces us to evolve a new way of thinking, or, as is the case with some folk, hurls us backward into dualism.

We can think of what is happening in the world currently (in 2022) as a kind of collective, global dark night of the soul. Not only did a pandemic upset the apple cart, but there is a growing rift between the right and left sides of the political world. In the United States, the government has become something run by big money factions and no longer representative of the will of the people. The Supreme Court, which was intended to be the impartial watchdog of the people's constitutional rights sitting in the judicial branch, has become a puppet of the executive branch and acts according to the politic of those who have appointed them. It just is a broken system and people on both sides are angry and upset.

So for many people, the beliefs with which they grew up, no longer work and no longer explain the reality of what they currently experience. Faced with that, they must either transform or fall back. Unfortunately, it appears that many have retreated to fundamentalism and dualistic thought (my camp and your camp). Many have retreated to fundamentalist religious beliefs and churches that peddle simplistic (right and wrong) morality. And that works (sort of)! If anything that we disagree with shows up, all we have to do is call it wrong and dismiss it.

But that is not transformative.

Returning to the theme of this chapter, what we must do—what we are continually challenged to do—is transform and grow. And the dark night experiences are the power tools of human transformation. Throughout my life, I can point to a series of events that were certainly dark nights—both personally and religiously. Each of these events—divorces, spiritual crises, deaths of loved ones, and immense failures—have pushed me further and further down the developmental path. Recalling (the process of re-membering, as was described in Chapter 4, as in putting back together) what happened in the darkness of those prolonged nights is the hard part and the source of my difficulty in regaining my full capacity to feel.

It does not have to be a crisis point-in-time that brings on the transformation. It could be, as Constance FitzGerald calls it, an impasse.[50] Think, for example of our African-American siblings who daily face discrimination and racism that is built into our policing, politics, and justice systems. It is not a single event (though I can only imagine the trauma of being pulled over in the night for no apparent reason other than my skin color). It is, rather, an ongoing and sometimes subtle undercurrent of their daily living experience, which seems insurmountable. It is a total impasse.

If we are not transformed by these experiences, the result is that we turn bitter and angered, railing against the situation or system that is oppressing us. In his classic text, *Pedagogy of the Oppressed*, Paulo Freire, says that this untransformed anger, in turn, tries to oppress the oppressor once (or if) it ever gains freedom from the oppression.[51] Put another way, my teacher and mentor, Richard Rohr is fond of saying, "What we don't transform, we will transmit."

---

50. Constance FitzGerald, "Impasse and Dark Night," in *Living with Apocalypse, Spiritual Resources for Social Compassion*, ed. Tilden Edwards (San Francisco: HarperCollins, 1984), 93-116.
51. Paulo Freire, *Pedagogy of the Oppressed: 50th Anniversary Edition* (New York: Bloomsbury Academic, 2018).

So when we encounter these dark nights and impasses, it is important for us to understand that they are how we are transformed and therefore to lean into the pain or suffering we are experiencing. When we sit in our suffering, we give it space to uproot and alter our core beliefs—almost, as it were, against our will. Our ego, or our conscious mind will want to escape, blame or duck and cover in reaction to such experiences. Ego does not want to be transformed–it is quite happy with the way it has figured things out. So it will not go down quietly, without a fight. And it is that internal struggle that eventually alters our core beliefs.

The conversation at the start of this chapter was the beginning of but one of my many dark night passages. When my young wife left me suddenly, it plunged me into what felt like a depression. But the dark night is dissimilar from depression because there once was something that one hopes will be rekindled. Depression is both hopeless and helpless. In the dark night, there is some vestige of hope in there. Not the hope that I could escape the feelings, nor a hope that some higher power would rescue me, but a hope based in the general belief that life is good—love is good. Somewhere along the line I had learned that it will all work out in the end—and if it has not worked out yet, this is not the end. I have always known myself to be the eternal optimist. Even in these dark nights, I held onto a fundamental belief in the goodness of life.

But that divorce was just the first of several events with which I felt out of control. There was the abrupt bankruptcy of the City University (my employer) that resulted in the loss of my first professional job. Years later, there was a second divorce—complicated by my own poor choices—that resulted in not only the loss of that marriage and custody of my two girls but also the loss of my job. It was not pretty, to say the least!

From the first divorce I matured slightly, while losing some of my naivety. The loss of the job in New York taught me resiliency. And through the second divorce I learned what commitment was and what integrity was. I finally began to learn how to honor my own word and live "as" my word.

But the really big dark night experience was a deep loss. I had opened a second franchised early childhood education center—based on the success of our first one. And while I was great at enrolling parents into sending their little ones to our school, the economic climate at the time meant that there were literally no experienced teachers on the market. The result was that I had to hire inexperienced young graduates who were not ready for the rigors of an academically oriented preschool (maybe they thought it was just a glorified baby-sitting gig!). The turnover was high and was not healthy for the children. It got to a point where I was facing a new influx of children and the loss of four of our teachers. And the result was that I would be critically out of the ratio of teachers and students mandated by the state.

We were faced with the decision to cut way back to the core of just two or three rooms (having to let go of most of the enrolled children) or we would have to close the center. Because our successful school was only seven miles away, we feared the negative impact of making the "Sophie's Choice" of who to send away and who to keep. So we decided that we would have to close.

Having spent time in the world of corporate outplacement, I knew the value of positive transitions and decided to outplace all of our children. I called every other local preschool and invited their directors or owners to come to the school and receive our kids. To facilitate that transition, I photocopied every child's records so that we could keep the obligatory files for us, and so that the other school could admit the student immediately without the hassle of gathering all that paperwork on its own.

Late that first night, I was alone in the office surrounded by mounds of files I was copying, when it hit me that they weren't just files. These were real children whom I had sworn to protect with my life, with whom I had already fallen in love. And that sudden realization was so hard-hitting that I burst into tears. I was sobbing uncontrollably and had to stop working. I cried the whole way home and ran into the bedroom and just wailed into the pillows—the pain and heartache were just unbearable! I fell asleep, exhausted, and the next day, I woke up feeling different. Something had changed—or perhaps it was more like something had opened up for me.

It was a wordless experience. It was, in fact, the experience of fully *experiencing* some feelings—not as thoughts or ideas but as pure emotions. I never knew how deep those emotions could go! But let me be clear here: While I have contended that emotions are often signals of what the emotion "wants" us to do, it is not necessary to immediately act on every emotion. In fact, sometimes it is the emotion that acts on us—and that action is what we refer to as transformation.

Nature is filled with the model of transformation. It is the natural order of things. On the simplest level we can think of it as order/disorder/reorder. But on a much deeper level, we call it birth/death/rebirth. Just look in a forest. You will see new sprouts shooting up through the decaying pieces of a dead tree. A seed falls to the ground and decays in the process of making a new plant.

We also see hundreds of examples of this same model of transformation in scripture. In the Hebrew scriptures the best examples are the stories of Job and Jonah. And in the Christian literature, the teacher Yeshua of Nazareth (Jesus) said that the only sign he would provide for those who needed a "sign" was that same story—the sign of Jonah (Matthew12:38 and Mark 8:12). What Jesus was referring to was the metaphor of going into the darkness of despair (the belly of the whale) and taken to the place we didn't want to go in the first place. In other words, the transformative path is often one that drags us, kicking and screaming, into the experience of having our reality ripped away from us (thus teaching us humility), only to be "spit out" on the shores of a new place where our humility will be of use.

What is truly funny about the Jonah story (I personally think it was written by some stand-up comic in ancient times) was that when Jonah preached the message of change to the people of Nineveh, they not only got it, but the king decreed that even the dogs should wear sack cloth and ashes! And of their immediate conversion Jonah shouts at God, "See I told you they would do it! You didn't need to send me. Oh just kill me now!" That just about sums up our surface reaction to the transformative dark night journey; oh just kill me now!

In the mythical story of Job we deal with the question of what happens when a really good and righteous person encounters a bad sequence of events. The story of Job is perhaps the oldest story in the entire *Bible*, predating even the writing of the book of Genesis, and as such is one of the classic human questions. Skipping all the detail, the bottom line of the Job story is that Job is angered at his bad luck and shouts to God that he wants his "day in court." It just is not fair, he protests, after all he has done everything right.

This goes on and on until Job finally gives up in an "oh just kill me" moment. It is only when he accepts his fate that God begins to talk with him. God points out the dark night theme—you are not in control and you never have been. You have no power over the forces of nature and nature is chaotic, unpredictable, and neither good nor bad. Nature just is. And we humans need to wake up and accept that, or the consequences will be suffering. As the Buddha taught, all suffering stems from wishing that our current reality would be or could be something different. But acceptance of the reality of chaos is the first step in the transformation process. We must realize that we (and our puny but stubborn little egos) are not in control. In fact, as Bill Wilson taught, we are "powerless" over our lives, over our circumstances, and over the chaos of the universe.

Given the benefits of transformation, most people would like the outcome; they just don't want to go down that path to get it. As a society, we have been taught that we do not have to deal with pain—there is a pill for that. We don't have to suffer; we can engineer that away. We can even prolong inevitable death. We are told by modern society that we deserve the "good life," which we assume means that we have all the goods without any of the hassles of getting there. We want that "beach body" or washboard abs without the discipline of exercise and proper nutrition. We want to have our cake and eat it too.

Sorry, that just isn't natural, nor is it the path of transformation. It is both difficult and unpleasant. We feel totally out of control, which might be the generic definition of suffering (anytime we feel like we have lost all control).

But who or what is it that wants control? Our lovely, self-constructed image of ourselves, which we call ego or self-image. Remember that the brain is our meaning-making organ. And from the very start, it works tirelessly not only to make sense out of the world around us but also of the internal world. It thinks, "I can do this and can't do that." It's the same function that early in our life as a child chooses either the "I'll show you" path or the "I guess I really am a nothing."

However, once having accumulated a pile of knowledge about what we are and are not, our brains want to keep that intact. It will resist anything that threatens to chip away at its well-constructed self-image. And that is exactly what the dark night passage—the path of transformation—does.

In dealing with this dark night—the loss of the business and of those beautiful children—I needed to talk. I am a social extrovert and I process things by talking it through with others. So I started talking to whomever would listen. Matthew was one of those who would listen.

"I feel like I have been turned inside out," I told him.

"Tell me more—what's coming up?"

"I feel like what has happened has caused me to be, well, more aware and sensitive. More aware of how I feel and what I feel. I am having feelings I have never experienced before."

"But that's your job—you're a psychologist, aren't you?"

"Yeah, but most of those emotions I put on the Periodic Table[52] were just words to me—until now. I feel like I actually can relate to them—like I know what they mean."

"You know," Matt continued, "this would make a great TED talk. Have you ever considered telling this story."

"Yeah, it's a fantasy of mine, but who wants to hear this?" I said with my old self-doubt taking the lead.

"Well, I would; I do," he persisted, "and I'd be willing to bet that a lot more people would want to hear it too."

Matthew was working as a volunteer at a local TEDx and volunteered to nominate me for an audition. To my amazement, they liked the story arc and I was in.

---

52. Matthew and I had previously talked about a training I had done for which I had created a table of emotions arranged like the Mendeleev elements table which I will discuss further in chapter 13.

Questions to Ponder:

1. What has transformed you (not changed, but reformed you)?

2. What experiences have ripped you open, most likely against your will, and how did you cope?

3. Take a moment to write down what your best TED talk might be. What would you talk about from your own experience that audiences might want to hear?

Part Four:
A Rainbow of Emotions

12

Naming Emotions

In our men's team, we were discussing how men cope with things in their life. Josh says rather matter-of-factly, "I get really pissed off when things don't go according to plan."

"Are you angry or frustrated?" I ask.

"They're both the same to me," he answers. "Don't you agree? I mean, what's the difference? They are both really negative reactions and only one punch apart!"

"I'm not so sure of that," I respond. "Is there some continuum from frustration to anger? Or might frustration be more about having an unfulfilled expectation, while anger might be more about relating to some wrong done to you or someone important to you?"

When Dr. Brené Brown started researching emotions over two decades ago, her original question was, "How many emotions can you name that you recognize when you feel it?" Here's the shocker though: the average number was three. Three emotions that we can recognize when we feel them—happy, sad and mad. And yet we know that there are hundreds, perhaps thousands of emotions we humans are capable of feeling. So maybe it's not so much that I and others are frauds in talking about emotions without a full understanding of their meaning and impact. Maybe that is the human condition. We feel stuff, but we are not fully aware or fully capable of identifying that which we are feeling.

The Ancient Greeks—specifically Aristotle—gave us our first peek into the world of emotions. Aristotle called emotions the drivers of human behavior and divided them into those that drive toward joy or those that are caused by or meant to avoid pain. But the thought that they were innate elements of the human nature started there. And that pretty much charted the course until some twenty centuries later when, in 1872, Darwin published his treatise on Human Emotions (*The Expression of The Emotions in Man and Animals*[53]).

From the time of Darwin, we have believed that emotions were innate reaction patterns that resided in sections of the brain. Darwin divided the brain into three brains: the reptilian brain, the mid-brain, and the cortical brain, ascribing emotions to the mid-brain region.

Emotions, Darwin felt, are what differentiated us from reptiles, as was discussed in the previous chapter. More importantly, his classification of the three brains stood firm and was embellished by psychology, most notably by William James, the father of psychology (who gave the name "limbic brain" to the mid-brain) and then by the field of psychiatry (brain medicine), all the way up to about two decades ago. That entire time we were looking for areas of the brain that controlled our senses and our emotions. We were looking for evidence of "wired patterns" from the perspective of an electro-physical or mechanical model that would confirm Darwin's theory.

But recently there was a breakthrough in brain research. Over the last decade, brain science researchers like Lisa Feldman Barrett, whom I discussed in the opening chapter, have been able to watch the brain "light up" as different processes are activated. And we found something startling: The brain is a vastly complex fluid process wherein the entire brain, spine, and body are often involved in processing different issues. And more surprisingly we are finding that there is no fingerprint or specific location or map for emotions. In other words, even strong emotions like love and hate and anger light up in different places with different individuals. This breakthrough exploded what we thought we knew about emotions. To make matters more complex, emotions are not singular in nature. That is, there are many types of anger just as there are many types of love, gratitude, joy, and passion (just to name a few).

What Barrett and her team found next has changed the game: Not only are emotions not relegated to certain patterns or areas of the brain but emotions are not even hardwired in us at birth. Emotions are constructions of the brain based on a very complex pattern of associations that are unique to each person. Basically, there are three types of construction:

---

53. Charles Darwin, *The Expression of The Emotions in Man and Animals*, 4th ed. (London: Oxford University Press, Anniversary edition, 2009).

- Social construction: Emotions are defined by and constructed around language and culture. In other words while we all smile when happy or cry when sad, what makes us happy or sad varies by culture and language.

- Psychological construction: This is what I discussed in the first chapter where the core systems (the intrinsic systems) of the brain which are continually processing somatic information, external stimulation and stored memories and sensations. All of that combines to create some kind of evaluation which is then projected into the next moment or into the future.

- Neuroconstruction: wherein emotions are the result of experiences essentially rewiring and hardwiring the brain.

And why that is important is that we now must rethink how emotions are "made." What this breakthrough means is that emotions are not the same for any two people because how we construct our emotional reactions is based on the experiences we have, the culture of our family and social group, our physical bodies and somatotypes, and ultimately the projections our brains make from those experiences.

Let me review how this mostly works: We see something happening and our brain scours the memory banks to find a context for meaning—anything that is like what it is that we are currently experiencing. It does not have to be that exact incident or person or place. The brain learns and recalls by association (this is *like* that). Oh, and just parenthetically, if that memory or context had an associated physiological state associated with it, that is remembered as well. Then, in the same instant, our clever brains project into the future (both near term and distant) about what that could mean and ascribe a valence to it. That energy is what triggers our endocrine reaction and the emotion that we experience. This all happens so rapidly, however, that you feel like you have an emotional reaction to that which is happening, not to the projection. How this happens may be the key to enhancing our ability to become more "emotionally intelligent" and more "emotionally responsive."

Now just to be fair, I am not 100% on the Lisa Barrett bandwagon. There is substantial research demonstrating that infants seem to have two innate fears: the fear of falling and the fear (or startle reaction) of loud noises. Conversely, there is not substantial data to indicate that *all* babies laugh and experience joy, but generally we do see most babies giggling, cooing, and laughing without having a context for why. So perhaps some of our emotions are hardwired in the medulla (reptilian brain), which might explain their role and power.

On the adult side of things, I am absolutely certain that a mother, who has carried her growing fetus inside her, then goes through the pain and agony of labor and delivery, absolutely dissolves into a pool of pure love the moment that newborn is placed on her chest. And irrespective of what her projections are at that moment, that is pure emotion. Furthermore, I am equally certain that what I feel, associate with, and project, on the basis of my loving experiences, is not the same as that mother's innate loving reaction. Emotions are both natural and built as well as being both common and individually unique.

Thus, part of understanding emotions will, of necessity, be learning how I built that substrate of information from which my brain is drawing its conclusions and projections. I needed to look at the cumulative effects of my past experiences, the impact of my family dynamics, and the social constructs in which I was steeped and matured. That has been a much deeper dive than I may have originally suspected. I had to recall what happened, and, perhaps more importantly, what interpretation I made of those events and those contextual situations in which I formed my self-concepts. That is where this is all headed and I will get there.

But that is only what is happening inside the mechanics of emotions. Externally we all needed a way to describe what we are feeling—or more accurately what it is we are having as a reaction—if I wished at all to engage with others or if I wished to become more emotionally intelligent. Now stick with me, here, because this is where it gets complicated. Brené Brown, in one of her famous TED talks, says, "What we know from the data is that the ability to accurately name an emotion helps us move through it, helps us heal, [and] helps us replicate it for the positive emotions." But, she continues, *"We just don't have a vocabulary that is as expansive as our human experience."*[54]

Here's where it got interesting for me. As a leadership coach, I started to fold emotional intelligence into my work with executives. Leaders don't simply lead because they are in the position. Nor do they come equipped with a substantial understanding of human psychology, irrespective of their B-School training. So my clients needed some better tools for leading and managing the team or company. They needed to know how emotions affected performance and the team. I began to search for different naming schemes. Who had done this work and what had they come up with? How were we to think of emotions? Were they on some sort of continuum or gradient of intensity or were they discrete, one from the other? What I found was that it is a little of both.

What I found was that most of the classification systems seemed to be organized around some of the more easily identified emotions and listed as gradients of those core ones. One list, not included here, was simply a list of emotion names in alphabetical order. That wasn't too helpful. There were lists and categories, t-shirts with emoticons, and overly simplistic categorizations of feelings. Some debated the difference between feelings and emotions

---

54. Brené Brown explains the misconceptions around guilt and shame, ABC News Australia, December 1, 2021, https://www.abc.net.au/news/2021-12-02/brene-brown-ted-talk-emotions-shame-guilt-misconceptions-covid19/100669362?utm_campaign=abc_news_web&utm_content=link&utm_medium=content_shared&utm_source=abc_news_web

One extensive but more recent list, created by Tom Drummond, an educator in early childhood development, listed 480 emotion words categorized as light, medium, and strong across 11 main categories. He said that he avoided simple names like mad, sad, and angry, partly because we all know what those are, and partly because they are gross generalizations of an array of other emotions. Drummond says he created his list simply by perusing the dictionary and writing down any emotion word he found, then placing them in a 10x3 matrix. Nice but lacking context.

I have only mentioned Drummond's chart[55] to show how extensive some lists can be. If you would like to learn more about Tom or this list and how he uses it with children and in teaching teachers, see his website at https://tomdrummond.com.

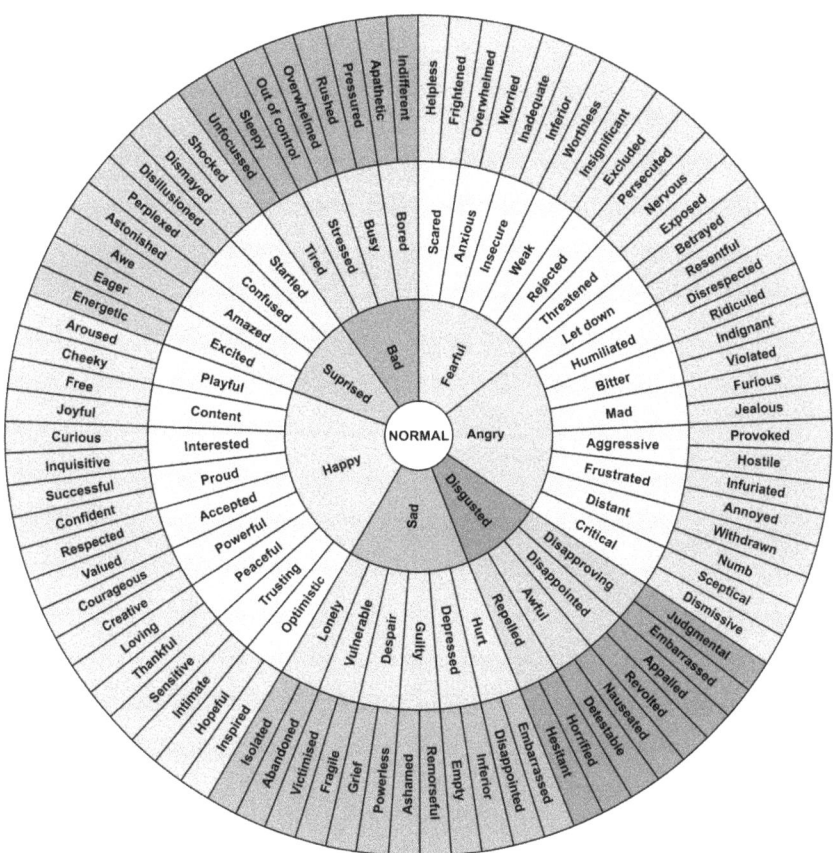

Most psychologists point to the original maps of emotions created by psychologist Robert Plutchik.[56] Plutchik created the simple pie-chart array of emotions shown above that demonstrates the relational nature of emotions but doesn't include very many emotion

---

55. https://tomdrummond.com/wp-content/uploads/2019/11/Emotion-Feelings.pdf

56. Robert Plutchik. "A General Psychoevolutionary Theory of Emotion," in *Theories of Emotion*, eds. R. Plutchik and H. Kellerman, *Theories of Emotion* (New York: Academic Press, 1980), Vol.1: 3-33.

names. He arranged his emotion chart such that opposite positions on the array were emotion families that could not be held at the same time. For example you cannot feel ecstasy and grief at the same time, or loathing and admiration simultaneously. Plutchik also contended that those emotional fields that were contiguous were in some way related, which I found a bit more of a stretch to understand!

The other often-cited lexicon of emotions is the emotion wheel first created by Gloria Wilcox at the Gottman Institute.[57] The version shown below is a third or fourth generation adapted from the Wilcox wheel, which was created by Mike Bostick[58] using a more Americanized vocabulary of previous iterations.

The Bostock/Wilcox Emotion Wheel contains one hundred thirty emotions arranged in seven major groupings. While many of the contiguous neighbors on the wheel are somewhat related—or at least the case could be made for that—some seem totally unrelated. I present these three models, not so much so you can see them (please feel free to look them up), but to acknowledge the various ways in which emotional vocabularies have been thought of in the past research.

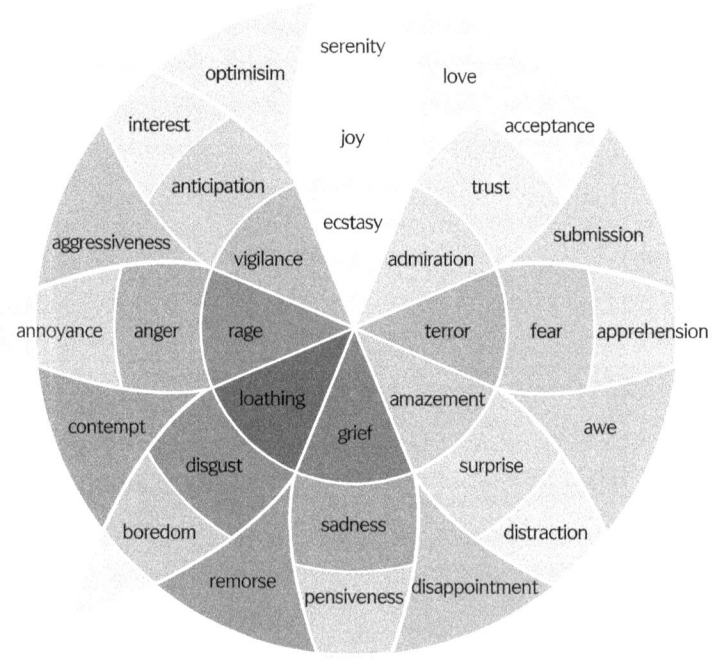

---

57. Gloria Wilcox, "The Feeling Wheel," *Transactional Analysis Journal* 12, no. 4 (1982): 274-276.
58. Mike Bostick, "Emotion Wheel," May 3, 2018, https://observablehq.com/@mbostock/emotion-wheel.

The bottom line here is twofold. First of all, these emotional charts were created well after I had graduated and gone off to seek my fortune as a counselor/coach. They were not part of either my education growing up nor of my professional training.

However, it was clear that these emotions and emotional experiences were something I had better learn more about before going further on my quest of understanding them. For me to figure out where my emotions came from, I needed to look back at my history.

Secondly, I wanted to find a way of classifying and organizing emotions that made sense to me. Something in the way they were organized just didn't click with my own experience. So I took a different path. Rather than organizing along families, I wanted to show relationships among all of the emotions but try to create a way that they might be organized by levels of complexity across a gradient of visceral or somatically experienced emotions to more ethereal and mentally experienced feelings. To begin with, I must admit that I am a latecomer to the party. So even after I had gotten the bug to learn more of emotions and emotionality, it was a) a theoretical pursuit and b) not really based in empirical research. To be certain, I started with Plutchik and Wilcox and by looking for as many emotion words from which I could sample. But my organizing structure took a different, more creative course, as I will explain.

However, something about what I had created struck a chord as witnessed by the 400,000 views of my TEDx talk on emotional intelligence. I am regularly asked for permission to use the Table (in the following chapter) by groups ranging from neurosurgeons to military leaders, priests, and educators.

Questions to Ponder

1. How many emotions can you name, and how many of those named have you fully experienced?

2. Think of a time when you found out that what you thought you had experienced was not at all like what others around you perceived. What was it like?

3. Which of your emotions do you feel less fully than others? Which do you feel more intensely? Make a list of your experienced emotions and the ones that you only "think you feel."

13

A Periodic Table of Human Emotions

Returning to the primary question at the start of the previous chapter: Do we look at emotions as analog or discrete? The periodic table, shown below, is an attempt to blend those two concepts. The organization right to left and left to right as well as from top to bottom is an analog-relational system, which is then overlaid with separate and somewhat individual and discrete emotions. But I did not create it out of thin air!

There are perhaps thousands of emotions and thousands of words we could use for our descriptions of how we are feeling, projecting or reacting to in any particular moment. So, I felt a need to build a vocabulary for those emotions with which we describe similar sets of experiences with similar words and I started with Plutchik and Wilcox. I had developed an interest in emotional intelligence but wanted to get better at understanding emotions in the first place. And that was the beginning of coming to *The Periodic Table of Human Emotions* as a way for me to talk about emotions.

I actually created the periodic table out of necessity a while back when I faced the daunting task of teaching emotional intelligence (EI) to a group of R&D managers in a pharmaceutical firm. The team were all highly educated, many with a doctorate in one discipline and an MD or other terminal degree as additional horsepower. However, despite their advanced educational levels, most had what I might call a "binary" emotional vocabulary. That is, if asked how they felt, their response was either "good" or "bad" or some variation on those two. And when I pushed further, they could name a dozen or so emotions, but the bottom line was they did not have an extensive lexicon of emotions (See my TEDx talk, "How we've been misled by 'Emotional Intelligence'" referred to in the previous chapter).

But if EI was based on the four factors of self-awareness, self-management, social awareness, and relationship management (a concept originally attributed to John Mayer and Peter Salovey[59] and later popularized by Daniel Goleman), we could not get to square one without having or expanding the ability to differentiate among various emotions. If a manager simply lumped frustration in with anger under the general heading of "bad feelings," their ability to manage that relationship might not be on very solid ground. So I had to create something that showed the variety of emotional words and showed some level of periodicity or relatedness—that is one emotion was like those to the right or left, but also somewhat different.

I believe that emotions are both relative (variants of other similar emotions) and discrete, one from the other (i.e., anger is not the same feeling as frustration). They are often similar in some ways but different in others. So, I started by arranging emotions on a chart with the lighter and purer emotions to the top and the heavy and somewhat unstable emotions at the bottom. Then the emotions were arranged from the more visceral, gut-level feelings toward the left moving to the more heady and spiritual emotions on the right. In order to put the whole discussion into a visual display that these scientists could relate to, I adopted the format of Mendeleev's Periodic Table of Elements—that chart we all had to learn in high school chemistry class (and shown on the following pages).

However, here is the thing you must know: *The Periodic Table of Human Emotions* is made up! Even though it, hopefully, makes sense, it is not based on research nor vetted against any standard. It was developed to get my scientists into the conversation about emotions and to teach them how to recognize emotional differences by having a more diversified language about emotions. And it was something I made up based on only those emotions and emotion names I knew of. Despite that, I had to leave out some because they just didn't fit my purpose.

To make the exercise a bit more fun and enticing to the scientists who had a healthy disdain for such "fluff," I gave each emotion a chemical symbol and an atomic weight (again, totally made up). Then, I built in puns and visual jokes to the table. For example Love, which, even though I consider it to be the purest of emotions wasn't placed in the first position so that I could give it the weight of 3.14 (pi) because love makes the world go round! Gratitude has the atomic weight of 24.7, as it should be our constant practice. Pleasure was given the chemical symbol Mm, Relief was given Rx, like some prescription, and Speechless was given the symbol Au because silence is golden. Empathy is all about you (U), Confusion is represented as thinking (Hm), while Dread has the unbelievable weight of 6×10^{26} (which in metric tons, represents the estimated weight of the world). Hurt was Ow, and Disappointment was a bummer (Bm). Denial doesn't believe it has any weight so none is listed. There are many more puns and jokes built into the Table but

---

59. P. Salovey and J. D. Mayer, "Emotional Intelligence," *Imagination, Cognition, and Personality*, 9 (1990): 185–211.

there are just as many whose symbols are just abbreviations of the emotion word or have atomic weights because of their position relative to other emotions. You will have to test yourself to find the puns or jokes! But they aren't the point. The point is that emotions are relative *and* discrete and that it is handy to have a way to identify emotions and their nuances by name and relativity to their neighbors.

And to reiterate, there are hundreds of human emotions (as in Drummond's list) and this list is not meant to be inclusive of everything or just the most important of emotions. They are just the ones I could fit in the chart in order to serve my purpose.

So enjoy it, use it, pass it on to others, but don't take it too seriously. Emotional Intelligence is a big and very important topic that requires a good deal of work. I admire and respect the work of other psychologists—both researchers and trainers—in the field of EI. I commend you to their work and employ it myself as a coach and trainer. But we have a long way to go in learning how to manage ourselves and be emotionally responsive and responsible in our relationships. My hope is that this Table will be just a simple and fun way to start that journey!

On the following pages I have included the Periodic Table, in two parts, mainly because in trying to put it all in one place, the print was too small to read. One way to get started might be to take the pdf of the Table[60] to a copy shop that has a large format printer and make a poster of it for yourself. Then adopt the practice of looking at the chart from time to time to see if you have uncovered any new or deeper understanding of emotions on the Table.

It's okay to disagree with the names of the emotions in the chart, their placement relative to each other, or to the underlying premise on which the table is created. That isn't the point. The point was twofold: (1) I had found a group of people who had less of a handle on their emotions than I had, and (2) putting the chart together forced me to learn more about how I conceived of and experienced my emotions. If you are similar to many others, the chart can be a fun or at least an entertaining place to start.

Another way to have fun and be light-hearted about the understanding of emotional experiences is to use the Table in playing a game of charades. Team A picks an emotion from the chart, taking note of the clues in the atomic weight or chemical symbol. Then one member of that team will attempt to act out the emotion so that Team B gets it within the three-minute time limit. This will really challenge understanding the experience of the emotion and not simply the feeling's name. You will be surprised by how wildly different people's definitions and descriptions or actions are represented.

---

60. For a free copy of the Table in PDF form, contact the author at kris@innerworks-consulting.com or by writing to 1 Meadowbrook Drive, Andover, MA 01810.

A Periodic Table of Human [Emotions]

Kris Girrell

Joy 1 **J** 1.001									
Love 3 **L** 3.141	Adoration 4 **A** 4.000								
Compassion 11 **C** 22.19	Empathy 12 **U** 22.222								
Happiness 19 **Ha** 32.021	Giddiness 20 **Gd** 33.333	Playfulness 21 **Pf** 33.950	Creativity 22 **Cv** 35.101	Awe 23 **Oo** 38.838	Reverence 24 **Rv** 39.222	Spirituality 25 **St** 40.000	Worthiness 26 **Wo** 42.012	Beloved 27 **Lv** 48.111	Satisfaction 28 **Ys** 49.019
Optimism 38 **Op** 57.001	Enthusiasm 39 **En** 58.100	Exhilaration 40 **Eh** 59.782	Sexiness 41 **Sx** 60.001	Sensuality 42 **Sn** 62.420	Pleasure 43 **Mm** 62.555	Innocence 44 **In** 63.141	Anticipation 45 **Aa** 64.995	Longing 46 **Ln** 68.241	Speechless 47 **Au** 69.002
Lethargy 57 **Lr** 93.041	Disappointment 58 **Bm** 96.096	* Passion 59-73	Frustration 74 **Fr** 152.44	Exasperation 75 **Ep** 151.86	Anxiety 76 **Ax** 158.22	Fear 77 **Fe** 169.01	Terror 78 **Tr** 174.97	Shock 79 **Sk** 178.48	Shame 80 **Sh** 180.95
Unhappiness 90 **Uh** 200.01	Sadness 91 **Sa** 201.86	** Depression 92-106	Grief 107 **Gf** 202.89	Pessimism 108 **Ps** 205.11	Boredom 109 **Bd** 205.68	Envy 110 **Ev** 210.55	Anger 111 **An** 211.22	Agitation 112 **Ag** 215.95	Aggravation 113 **Av** 220.88

* Passion Series

Rapture 59 **Ra** 98.600	Infatuation 60 **In** 99.999	Lust 61 **Lu** 100.00	Obsession 62 **Ob** 104.02	Desire 63 **De** 110.01	Arousal 64 **Ar** 121.212	Jealousy 65 **Jl** 124.241	Rejection 66 **Re** 132.99

** Depression Series

Melancholy 92 **Ml** 1001.0	Withdrawal 93 **Wd** 1010.0	Isolation 94 **Ii** 1011.0	Abandonment 95 **Ab** 1100.0	Lost 96 **Ls** 1101.0	Despair 97 **Ug** 1221.12	Devastation 98 **Ono** 1348.0	Emptiness 99 **Ep** 1500.0

Copyright© 2010, 2022, Kristen W Girrell, all rights reserved

...man Emotions

								Peace 2 **P** 1.111
			Blessing 5 **B** 4.41	Bliss 6 **Bl** 5.001	Delight 7 **Dl** 5.555	Contentment 8 **Ah** 10.000	Humor 9 **Ho** 11.001	Hope 10 **H** 12.365
			Solemn 13 **So** 23.001	Reflection 14 **Rf** 23.876	Gratitude 15 **Gr** 24.700	Elation 16 **El** 28.960	Excitement 17 **Ex** 29.501	Ecstasy 18 **X** 30.000
Humility 29 **Ge** 50.050	Pride 30 **Pr** 51.600	Grace 31 **Gc** 52.050	Astonishment 32 **As** 52.995	Amazement 33 **Az** 53.010	Surprise 34 **Su** 54.000	Jubilation 35 **Ju** 55.555	Cheer 36 **Ch** 55.950	Eagerness 37 **Ea** 56.950
Bravery 48 **Bv** 71.000	Impatience 49 **Im** 72.727	Determination 50 **Dt** 77.777	Confusion 51 **Hm** 78.257	Distant 52 **Ds** 79.001	Comfort 53 **Cm** 80.008	Nostalgia 54 **N** 84.123	Tranquility 55 **Tq** 88.888	Relief 56 **Rx** 90.000
Vulnerability 81 **Vu** 183.84	Exposure 82 **Ed** 188.89	Disgrace 83 **Dg** 191.02	Humiliation 84 **Hu** 192.66	Hurt 85 **Ow** 192.86	Embarrassment 86 **Em** 195.0	Remorse 87 **Rm** 197.23	Contempt 88 **Co** 198.96	Guilt 89 **Gu** 199.99
Tension 114 **Tn** 228.28	Stress 115 **Ss** 232	Apprehension 116 **Ap** 245.01	Doubt 117 **Db** 257.11	Hesitation 118 **Hs** 277.11	Homesick 119 **Hk** 285.21	Loneliness 120 **Lo** 291.01	Grouchiness 121 **Os** 296.22	Denial 122 **Dn**

Resentment 67 **Rs** 138.91	Bitterness 68 **Bt** 140.01	Loathing 69 **Lg** 141.29	Hatred 70 **Ht** 144.99	Wrath 71 **Wr** 145.01	Fury 72 **Fu** 148.28	Rage 73 **Rg** 150.96
Worthlessness 100 **Wt** 1929.0	Depression 101 **Dp** 2000.1	Misery 102 **Ms** 2290.1	Hopelessness 103 **Hl** 2470.1	Gloom 104 **Gm** 2525.1	Dread 105 **Dd** 6.0×10^{24}	Numbness 106 **Mu** 0000

Questions to ponder:

1. Of the four emotional layouts presented in this and the last chapter, which offers you the greatest access to understanding your own set of emotions, and what is it that you find more relatable about that format? (And it's okay if you don't pick mine!)

2. Sit down with a friend or lover and discuss how each of you experience various emotions. What are similar and what are different?

14

Experiencing Emotions

"I call them the lost years," I said trying to get a handle on what happened after my second divorce. "I just immersed myself in another relationship that never should have happened."

"You can say that again," Sarah chuckled. "She was what, seventeen years younger than you? What were you thinking?"

"That's the point," I said, "I wasn't thinking. I just fell into it because it was there—she was there, and at least that was something that felt good. I didn't hurt so much when I was with her. But I don't think I ever once said 'I love you' to her."

This was such a repressed emotional experience that when I would try to fill out the places I had lived for the required CORI report as an owner of an early childhood education center, I could never make the places I'd lived match up with the number of years or months spent in each place. It just never computed.

How do we cope with these intense life situations if we do not have either an understanding of how emotions work—if we think we are being held hostage by our emotions—and if we have no way to describe what it is that is happening inside? More importantly, how was I dealing with my life situations when I had such a limited experience with emotions of my own? Perhaps I have been able to handle some of those complexities and intensities, but now I needed something else. Discovering our emotions comes basically in three steps as I mentioned earlier:

- First, we have the experience of our experience. This is simply allowing my body to have sensations of one or another type without classifying or labeling then. Often our emotional reactions are more our reactions to the sensations in our body than the specific emotions associated with the event. However, in either case, the entire brain is involved in making an interpretation of what is happening, as Barrett and her team have found.

- Secondly, we must understand (by recollection or through conversations with siblings and friends from those days) how we made interpretations of those events and what those interpretations were that now sit at the base of our meaning-making as an adult. If Sarah is correct (and I think she is), some of those interpretations and some of those events are still driving our behaviors, whether we like it or whether we are aware of them or not.

- And thirdly, we label our experience with some kind of emotion word that best describes it. Notice I did not say with the "correct" or "exact" name. What I have learned in this process is that it is all about trying on differing names and definitions to see if they fit our experience. For example, look up the differences between hurt, embarrassed, humiliated, and disgraced. Though each is similar in some way with the others, they are each slightly different in intensity, negativity, and interpretation.

Despite trying our best not to feel emotions on the negative side of things, we still experience them, and we seem to want to increase the occurrence of our positive and uplifting emotions. In general, we humans will do more to avoid pain than we will to maximize our pleasure. Unfortunately, one way we have chosen as a society to handle negativity is to drug it away or alter how it occurs. Look at the most prescribed drugs (for anxiety, hypertension, ulcers, depression, and pain). But I believe a far more effective way to deal with our emotional states would be to become more emotionally intelligent and self-aware. As I was processing some of these events in my past—the really negative ones—I noticed that I had chosen alcohol as my drug of choice at times. Though I would not consider myself to be alcoholic, that relationship with alcohol as a tool for numbing pain and negativity was not a healthy one and most likely contributed to my inability to recall them. It takes me (and anyone who does so) away from the experience of the experience and further disallows the full recognition of those feelings as well as our ability to deal with them. The consequences of not listening to your feelings, whether cognitive or somatic, can be significant, as I have found.

> I was running my fourth Boston Marathon in April of 2000. I hadn't really noticed that my time had slowed by a minute per mile over the last year—apparently the result of a bulging disc leaning on the nerve bundle that innervates my left leg. Somewhere around mile seventeen, in Newton Lower Falls, the disc exploded,

severing part of that nerve bundle. The searing pain that shot down my leg was unlike anything I had ever experienced, and I started limping and slowed my pace to a jog.

I had stationed my friend Bill at Newton town hall near the beginning of Heartbreak Hill, with a polypropylene shirt as it was a cold wet day. He saw me approaching.

"How are you doing?" he asked, holding out the shirt.

"Billy, something is terribly wrong! My leg won't work and I'm cramping like hell." I pulled on the shirt thankful for the extra layer of warmth.

Bill was an experienced runner and seemed to understand my situation. "I'll go with you up Heartbreak, and let's see it you can walk it off." So we headed up the first incline past Johnny Kelly's statue.

As we crested the summit, I tried jogging a little bit, but the pain only intensified. Bill encouraged me as I limped away, "Take it easy, and just jog," he shouted. And so I alternated between limping and slow jogging, right past the medical tent in Cleveland Circle, and like a fool, I finished the race in just under five hours. Never once did I have the thought that my body was telling me to stop. Though I tried to run the next day just to see if I could shake off the cramping, I was not able to. My left calf atrophied in a matter of three months and ended with surgically removing the disc. As a result, I still walk with a permanent limp. And I have not been able to run since that day.

Not listening to our feelings and emotions can result in the loss of friendships, the loss of sleep, emotional (and even physical) harm to ourselves and others. Emotions are messages from our body and our mind—both of which are intricately bound together. They serve as a kind of early warning system for what we are experiencing. But when we deny their existence, we may have to pay the price.

Emotional Intelligence, in its simplest description, is the ability to recognize emotional experiences in ourselves and others so that we are able to talk about them, and perhaps to manage our reactions (and projections) we have in certain situations, resulting in a better understanding of what we should do. As an athlete running for a charity, I was determined to finish and honor my commitment, but that drive blocked out my ability to rationally process my feelings and responsiveness. On the other side of the table, EI does not mean recognizing another's emotional state correctly but instead asking them for what they are experiencing and being able to respond appropriately to their emotions in a way that supports them.

The key to effective emotional intelligence is to be aware enough of our own emotions, our own drivers, and beliefs so that we will not view someone else's experience through our own lens. What that means is that we must be clear on what is ours and what is the other person's experience. The best way to do that is by simply asking what they are experiencing. We don't even ask what the emotion name is (that most likely is our own need). Learning how to distinguish our emotional experience and name it is for us. But in that other part of EI, we must provide the space and acceptance to allow them either to name their experience as they see it and accept—really believe—their description as it is.

Think back to an intense emotional experience you have had. It may have been an instant (for example, a car suddenly pulling out in front of you causing you to slam on your brakes in order to avoid it) or a building or slow onset (such as an intensifying argument). As you recall one of these situations, notice how your body felt. Emotions, specifically emotional experiences, always have a physical component. Sometimes the physical sensation elicits the emotion (like when you are falling), and sometimes the physical response follows the emotion, such as when we are in an argument. But the fact remains that emotions always have both a physical and a mental/cognitive aspect to them.

> In Nepal we were on a trail that at one point crossed a high river gorge. Spanning the gorge was a metal suspension bridge that was quite safe and well-built, but seemed rather scary to me, not only because of the height but because the treads that made up the walkway had holes allowing you to see through them. As I approached the bridge, my pulse started quickening (I have always had an unexplained fear of heights). But stepping onto the bridge accelerated that. My hands were clammy, my breathing was shallow and rapid, and my heart rate had to be over 150 BPM! These are the physiological manifestations of fear. So, while my mind was racing with "ohmygod, ohmygod, I'm gonna die" both my body and mind were jointly producing an increasingly higher level of fear that rose with each successive step. On the other side of the river, I sat down to compose myself. I felt relief despite the fact that my heart was still pounding and my hands were still wet with sweat. However, the effect of feeling relief (mentally knowing I was no longer in danger) was to reduce the physiological responses which in turn furthered the calming effect.

In other words, while we may experience our emotions as unitary events or experiences, they result in a whole slew of mind/body experiences. Those intense experiences—being robbed at knife point, surviving an accident, being screamed at by some outraged friend or customer or crossing over a high gorge—often seem to blend into one event. When we attempt to remember the fear, the anger, or our life flashing before us, we tend to forget or gloss over the complexity of what was happening in that moment. So naming our emotions further reduces the complexity of what happened into a single word or name.

That may explain why once we have emotional words, we still feel hesitation or even trepidation around using them. Most of us have not been trained on understanding our emotions or on how they are created or are used. And because we don't have that same depth of understanding that we have, let's say, for our career subject matter, we still resist naming or using our emotions to their fullest.

As a coach and counselor, I was always taught (and subsequently have always taught my protégés) to "let the silence do the heavy lifting."[61] But, when we coaches are doing that, it is more for the effect of intensifying the thought process and emotions for our clients. As coaches, we are not processing the information—our insight is relatively meaningless to the client. The silence, however, is uncomfortable for them and results in pushing their thought process further down the field. With my friend Andy who is informally a teacher of mine, silence is an active and participative experience. He is listening and then listening to his listening, then allowing his inner being to react cleanly to what he has experienced in that listening. There is a lot going on, and as the other half of that conversation, it is clear to me and provides space for me to do the same.

Experiencing emotions is more than just the ability to name a feeling. It is more than the recognition of the preceding thought that may have triggered the emotion, though, to be certain, it is imperative that we become aware of the role of our thoughts and interpretations. Experiencing emotions or more accurately experiencing the experience of those emotions is a whole-body experience that brings a greater depth of personal awareness to our experience, to our understanding of what is really going on and to our ability to react fully and cleanly to that.

Questions to ponder:

1. What experiences have you had that are most difficult to recall? What was the nature of those experiences and feelings?

2. How do you separate feelings that are somewhat to very similar? What different names might you give them?

3. What marks the difference between feeling and experiencing the experience of a feeling for you?

---

61. Something I learned from Susan Scott, author of *Fierce Conversations: Achieving Success In Work and Life One Conversation at a Time* (New York: Penguin Group, 2002).

15

Learning Compassion

These days (in 2022), we are experiencing a time of international crisis, so forget that I have studied this field of emotions, psychology, theology, and all that. Today, I am just another person trying to cope with the changes and uncertainty that we all are facing: a war that threatens to escalate to the unthinkable at any moment, the continuance of a global pandemic that mutates to fight whatever our scientists can concoct to build our resistance to it, and climate changes that result in drought, famine, intensified hurricanes, and the foreboding death rattle of our host planet.

I would like to address some of the deep emotions that may be coming up for many of us during this time of grave uncertainty. In the chapter on *Impasse, Failure, and Transformation*, I discussed how that process of hitting an impasse strips away our egoic willfulness and causes us to develop to the next level. It is not hard to look around our current state and recognize that for the greater part of the world, we are in such a place—an impasse that seems to be beyond our control, locally, nationally, and globally.

The current situation is producing a somewhat similar "dark night" effect. People (you and I) feel frustrated, scared, angry, and even depressed. Nothing we knew has fully prepared us for dealing with this. Oh, certainly there have been a dozen apocalyptic movies about viruses where the hero/heroine had too little time to find the remedy before the human race was eliminated. And there is that 2015 TED talk by Bill Gates that seems so prophetic now. But the bottom line is that we (our countries, the World Health Organization, and each of us personally) were not prepared for this pandemic, nor have we even begun to recognize the full ramifications of it. And then the overlay of a war involving at least one nuclear power tilts the balance into overwhelming. We are often left thinking, "What can I do about it other than cover my own ass and worry about my family?" So in this chapter, I would like to discuss one of the by-products of the dark night passage.

What psychology and theology have learned about dealing with impasse and feelings of being totally trapped inside our own experience is that it actually produces a state of pain—various forms of pain like mental anguish, fear, frustration, anger, disillusionment, and despair—but pain in every sense of the word. We actually feel these emotions physically in our bodies and minds. And over the centuries of studying and working with these painful impasses, the sages of our professions have come to a few conclusions about how to "deal" with impasse and the dark night phenomenon.

The first and foremost of these suggestions (as it were) is that we need to be able to sit with the pain and discomfort. If we are unable to be present to the pain and the physical reality of impasse, we will tend to deny what is really happening and become unable to do a thing about it. In other words, ducking and covering our heads in an attempt to wait it out, or numbing and drugging it away not only creates further pain, but it renders us helpless and clueless about what to do. When, however, we recognize our pain as a reality, we are able to begin to heal it. What we need is compassion.

The second insight is that the dark night is the birthplace of compassion. But that compassion has to start with ourselves. We must get to a level of self-worth and self-acceptance where we can embrace the pain and despair fully—without denying it. This is not a matter of "cowboying up" and toughing it out. It is, instead, a time to be gentle with yourself, to allow yourself to feel the pain and meet it at its source. Self-love and self-care are to be administered with the same tenderness that you would give your ill child.

The amazing thing about suffering with and through pain is that it gives you access and understanding to that reality. This is the most important lesson of suffering: You cannot give compassion to others if you do not know suffering on your own part or have not practiced compassion for yourself first. Anything you try to do as compassionate without your own caring self-compassion will be patronizing and coming from privilege. No one wants to be patted on the head and told "Oh, poor thing, this will pass," by someone who has no clue of what pain and suffering actually feels like.

Granted, you have felt pains before. That is not the question. Did you allow yourself to experience the pain, the hopelessness inside that pain, and did you find a way to comfort yourself in that place? That is practicing self-compassion. So how will you deal with this learning moment in world history? Will you let in the fear, despair, and pain enough to learn how to self-soothe? Or will you try to be the hero and provide comfort to others without knowing what it really means to feel and experience the fear, panic, helplessness, and the whole raft of other emotions that emerge from it?

There is an additional and very important distinction about learning self-compassion, that is, through this process of feeling the pain and suffering, you will become very clear that no one can know exactly what you are going through. It is unique to you. So when we translate that outwardly, we now understand that having compassion for others is not saying that we "understand" their pain. What we have learned is that each of us has our own unique experience. What we can do—and what true compassion is—is to be present with that other person, to listen to their experience, to believe them when they tell us how painful or difficult it is. *That* is compassion!

But why must we learn compassion in the first place? Well over one third of the seven billion members of the human race live at the margins or well below a level of subsistence. Those people living in the shadows and on the margins of society normally have to live with this uncertainty (about where the next meal might come from, about dealing with death and illness with no visible means of healing) on a continuing basis. This latest global crisis throws them further into the abyss. This is a teachable moment, as it is called in education. It is a time rife with lessons and it is incumbent on us, as leaders, to be aware and learn what is here to learn. This is a time to learn compassion, if ever there was such a time.

It is not just some nice thing to do. There is a major chunk of responsibility that comes with learning to feel, and that is that once you have begun to experience the fullness of those emotions, you will start to see into other humans' emotions, their suffering, their joys—all of it. This trip of learning how to feel comes with some baggage. You cannot shut off the feeling for some things without shutting it off for all things without effecting your ability to fully feel and experience all things. Likewise you cannot open up to experiencing the fullness of some emotions without opening up to all of them. Either way it's a package deal.

That can suck! Our minds want to keep things conveniently controlled and manageable. The only analogy I can think of is to a dog's ability to smell. It is said that a dog's sense of smell is about 1,000 times stronger than a human's. What if suddenly you had the ability to smell like that? You might feel overwhelmed because you could smell when someone was feeling fear. You could smell foods being cooked in a kitchen a mile away. You could know who you could trust and who you couldn't just by how they smelled.

Turning on your sense of feeling is like that. Suddenly you may find yourself feeling the pain of others in your community. When a tragedy happened, you would not be "sending your thoughts and prayers," you would be doubled over with grief and pain because it was all too intense. It's not that you were empathizing with them or "walking in their shoes" (you can't), but that you are experiencing the fullness of pain and suffering. You may not want this trip. But for me the alternative of not being able to experience my experience of feelings has proven to be too costly.

September 11th, 2001 I was conducting day two of a leadership development training for a global firm in our area. The workshop exercise had just begun when the president of the client organization came in to stop us saying that there was a national emergency. We all went out to the lobby of the hotel and watched the towers fall—over and over—as the news media, in as much disbelief as we were, kept showing what had happened. My boss had come earlier that day to see how the workshop was going since I had created a new and unique program we hadn't used before. I turned to him for guidance:

"What should we do now? These guys can't go anywhere or call anyone."

"I suppose we could offer that they could go over to the HQ (just about five miles from the training site), or we could offer to continue the workshop." A quick circle up of the participants yielded a vote for the latter.

Turning back to Mike, I asked, "And what about me? What am I to do? I know people in those buildings." (I had just completed a coaching project with a bunch of execs on the 14th floor of the North Tower, earlier that summer.)

"You are a professional—get back in there and run the workshop."

My jaw dropped. I was confused, angry, worried for our collective safety, and in short, overwhelmed. I hadn't been able to get a call out to anyone, not even my wife—the cell lines were all dead or overloaded. I turned to our staff psychologist, who had also come to observe the session, but the dazed look in her eyes told me that she hadn't the capacity to help me process my emotions either. I just was not ready to go back to the front of a room and lead another process.

I excused myself and went outside the hotel. In the back parking lot was a big dumpster that I leaned up against and started crying. Then, the rage came out, and I started pounding punching the dumpster until my knuckles were bleeding. It was cathartic, in some very healing way. This all happened, by the way, before my compassion had been fully awakened, some fifteen years later. But the force of that tragic event was sufficient to put me into a state of emotional awareness that altered my behavior.

Back in the room, we picked up where the workshop had been interrupted. We had been doing an exercise called "Corporate maze," a puzzle of one team versus another that involved movement across a grid on the floor according to an undisclosed map. Solving the puzzle required getting to a level of teamwork and cooperation with the opposing team (also an undisclosed rule). The only problem was that the participants just went back to playing the game as they had been doing before the attack.

I was out of my mind and fully in the swirl of my emotional state. I jumped up on a table and shouted at the top of my lungs, "*Wake the fuck up! In case none of you has been paying attention, somebody just changed all the rules! You cannot play the game the same as it was. You need to find a new way to be a leader right now, because this just won't cut it anymore."*

What followed was one of the most powerful and effective workshop sessions I had ever run. Now, I would not exactly consider my emotional outburst as either compassionate or emotionally intelligent—in fact, it probably wasn't even a bit professional. But the depth of pain and compassion I had experienced in witnessing the destruction on that day led me to be different than my normal self as a trainer and coach and it produced an outcome that was very impactful for the participants in that room.

Compassion is a powerful force and when it comes from a level of self-awareness and self-love. I felt compassion for the people and families involved in the 9/11 attack and was moved by that. But I perhaps did not experience the same level of compassion for the managers in my training, who I perceived had been numbed by the repetitive showing of the towers crumbling and people jumping to their death. Compassion can move us to action in ways we may never have considered.

Questions to ponder:

1. What pains are you unwilling to sit with? What do you fear might happen if you were able to just let it be painful for the moment?

2. Where and how have you learned compassion for yourself?

3. How do you process the depth of pain that humanity faces on a daily basis? Or do you?

Part Five:
Finding Emotions and Emotional Intelligence

16

The Red Thread

The "red thread" is an expression that comes either from eastern thought where it is often referred to as the "red thread of fate" or from our Scandinavian heritage where they would refer to the red thread as the blood line of thoughts—through which all other thoughts are related.

Everything that I (or we) experience and feel is tied in some way to our past learning and all of our other experiences. We can't really help that—we can only be aware of that. But once aware, we can effectively choose to respond rather than to react in our habituated way. And if I were to tell the truth, I am afraid that most of my actions in life were *re*actions, not actions or choices.

Here is a vivid example: I started the book relating a challenge from my partner Sarah to dig deeper into why I once flirted with an old flame despite my commitment to monogamy. If I were to look solely at the action to try and understand what my motivation was in that moment, it would be perhaps futile or at the very least not terribly productive. That singular look keeps the discussion on the surface level. But what is it about this one incident that ties into my past, my meaning-making, and my underlying needs and fears? What I needed to find was the red thread.

To dig under the surface, I engaged in a form of hypnotherapy called "Rapid Transformational Therapy" (RTT). Though it may not be transformational as a tool by the standards we in the field of transformational technology would view it, it is highly helpful in finding the thread that runs through a bunch of different experiences that set up the whole thing.

In signing up for the RTT session, I was originally seeking the source of my prostate cancer, based on the fact that I eat an extremely healthy diet, consisting of mostly organic vegetables and fruits, no processed foods, no flour or refined carbohydrates and no sugar. And yet I am totally aware that my body created the cancer—I didn't "catch" cancer. Cancer is not contagious or transmitted is some way between two people or organisms. It was my own system's dysfunction that created it. So if my food were not the source of the aberrations in cell mitosis, then perhaps the stress on my bodily systems could be the source. Or, was there some other source I had yet to uncover?

And so, the session began by reeling back time to a previous date where I may have some stuck energy. I was to sit quietly for a while and recall any stuck energy. I recalled a day when I was commuting to work in the City (NYC) shortly after my first wife had left me for another lover. I was in such pain and heartbreak I didn't think I could bear it, and I was staring out through the train window that rainy day. The tears running down my face were matched by the rivulets of rain streaking down the outside of the window. I felt alone, saddened, unlovable, and broken. I had wrapped myself around her and her career as a trailing spouse and suddenly felt abandoned.

But why should I have expected anything else? We had gotten married because as young college students, we figured (obviously, I thought) that having great sex meant we should get married, and right after graduation, we did. However, my young wife, a highly sought-after scientist, began traveling around the country for her work (as I discussed before). And her traveling companion was another young (male) scientist. It was not too long until they got together and found an equally exciting and fulfilling sexuality together. Her proclamation of "I'm leaving you for another man" followed shortly after.

Back in the RTT session, the therapist rewound the clock a few more years. The next memory up was that Bob Seger, *Night Moves* kind of experience with a neighbor girl, just exploring each other—not really full-out sex, but the touchy-feely stuff. We couldn't have been more than 13 or 14 at the time, and "I used her and she used me, but neither one cared," as Bob so eloquently put it. "We were gettin' our share." I was embarrassed to tell the hypnotherapist about this memory, but wanted to get all I could out of the process, so I was forthcoming with the scene. So it was a second, rather sex-related but hidden memory.

Once more, the therapist rolled back the clock to an earlier place in my childhood. In this scene, something I hadn't recalled in ages, I was being "talked to" by my mother because I had been caught with some of my father's *Playboy*-type magazines under my bed. My age at the time was perhaps 9 or 10. Mom was telling me that if I wanted to know anything about women or women's bodies, she would show me or tell me herself. I hope you can imagine the level of embarrassment I felt as a boy of ten—I simply did not want to know *that* about my mother, for God's sake!

Truthfully, I had never put those events in a line-up together. But what if sex and sexuality is the red thread that ties this all together? Is it possible that long-held guilt and shame about some elements of my sexuality eventually caught up with me and manifested in the disease in my prostate?

But holding those together as a unit also brings up another connection. What was it about a flirtatious email exchange, so many years later, that tapped into that same sexual identity thread? One clear theme that was a common thread was my hiding and not expressing the underlying feelings in each of these past events (were there more?). In fact, I was not simply hiding them; I was convinced that I did not know what I was feeling. There had been a knowledge of something "wrong" or at least unacceptable to the powers in my life who might judge those events. Compelled by my own desires, I had engaged in something that was destined not to work, something that I knew would not end well.

Even as I look back on my first marriage, I had a feeling that we were rushing in blindly. What I can finally see is that when my father died so suddenly, I shut down emotionally. I didn't want to feel those deeper emotions of grief and pain. So while I fell in love with my first wife and could experience that emotion—at least on the surface—I was not fully aware emotionally of what was going on either inside of me or in our relationship. And even if I was aware (which I was pretending not to be), I most likely had already learned not to trust my own emotions. But the wheels were already turning; I had been accepted to grad school in Boston and we would either need to get married (so that we could live in the married grad housing) or call it quits and go our separate ways. I chose the former out of fear of losing this rock star of a girlfriend. She would be famous someday (I was certain of that) and I wanted to ride along with that trip. Over the next two years our relationship just slid from one situation to another. And when she became disinterested in us or perhaps in me, I was oblivious. I could not perceive what was happening because those "senses" were still numbed. Having numbed out the negativity meant that I was also numb to any perception of "things going south" in the relationship.

There was also a second marriage—one that ended in divorce after ten tears—but again, I had a faint sense that I should not go through with it. While engaged to be married, I had another young woman invite me to go on a trip with her to Alaska. I was tempted but declined. Nonetheless, even being in enough of "another" relationship to have been invited should have told me that I was not fully invested in this one. Yet, the invitations had been sent, the priests and ministers had been alerted and scheduled, caterer hired and all the rest. I couldn't put a stop to that train, I thought. So there is another thread: knowing better and not doing what I knew I should. But I hadn't wanted to lose what looked to be a promising relationship.

Now, some forty years later, I had remarried for a third time and still had some of that residual denial or suppression of emotions. And once again I was operating out of fear: fear of not being loved or accepted as who I was, fear of abandonment, fear of losing out. Fear drives a thousand forms of problems. From it stems all kinds of disfunction and spiritual maladies, as Bill Wilson wrote in the *Big Book of Alcoholics Anonymous*. Driven by fear, we step on the toes of our dearest friends and loved ones. Because of fear, we rob our relationships of our full participation and withhold our gifts to our loved ones. When this is confounded by repression and denial of the negative side of things, it results in further harm. From the outside it looks as if I am not considering the impact and repercussions of my actions.

But why would I do that which would result in shame, guilt, and fear in the first place? For me it looks like I was more afraid of not being enough—enough of a loveable person, enough to warrant the love of another, enough to stand on my own—than I was of the consequences of doing what I ultimately felt was wrong in the first place. Was I just repeating the pattern to prove my negative self-limiting beliefs true? Was I acting as if I did not know how it would affect me and others? Suddenly, what Sarah had tried to pry out of me—why I did what essentially crossed the boundary of fidelity with my sexually oriented flirtations—makes more sense. I carry with me that form of shameful identity that would want to hide my actions from sight—mine and especially hers. And at the same time I carry a sense that my worth is only in my physical desirability to someone else, even if that someone else is not my marriage partner. But the bottom line is that I still act from that partially numbed sense of perception of the negative consequences of my actions, under the pretense of not knowing. It's deadly!

When it comes to our emotion-based actions, there is no real logic in place. Emotions are not logical. I was not being logical. Despite all of my training and all of my attempts to hammer the emotions out of decisions and actions, I had made irrational, but emotional choices that were driven by fear, insecurity, and avoidance, and compounded by a learned shame for who I am. Like the other slaves in *Spartacus*, I was acting on the emotion of the moment without any consideration of the effects of that action. I was fraudulent in not acting in a way I knew to be my calling.

So let's weave together this pattern. Sexuality (learned in the back woods and stirred by the foundations of poor-folk mentality) was a way to feel meaningful because of the radical nature of sex as an intimate expression of acceptance. Add to that having hammered flat many or most of my emotions as a result of not dealing or wanting to deal with such deep feelings as grief at my father's passing or the loss of my first marriage. Shame, on the other hand, (learned through religion and society) drove me to hide my actions from public view in general and, most specifically, from my wife with whom I had a promise of transparency.

Top those off with a healthy dose of education—an oh-so-nice way to disguise awareness—and we have a perfect storm. Through education, specifically the study of psychology, emotions, and theology, I had conveniently learned how to objectify and distance myself from the feelings themselves and pretend to be a casual observer of my own life. The only problem was that I was not particularly observant in seeing what my ego did not want to admit was there!

Through life experiences I had learned to hammer flat some of the intense feelings which resulted in a general lack of awareness of the full range of emotional experiences. However, those same heavy-duty experiences were the source of massive transformations. Through them I had evolved in my moral and ethical maturity. So they together represent the double bind of advanced thought without the associated emotional awareness that might normally accompany them.

One of my favorite questions I frequently use in coaching is, "What are you pretending not to know?" It is a powerful question because it is built on the understanding that the knowing is there but hidden by the pretense of not knowing it actually is there. When I ask myself that question about past actions, I am now able to answer. I was pretending not to know that there were consequences for every action or inaction. I was pretending not to know that I do not live life in some solitary fashion—that I am, in fact, in relationship with my wife, my family, my close friends and associates. Furthermore, I was pretending that I and my actions are not visible to others— strangers and friends—who, by virtue of the many forms of social media which I occupy, will also see what I am doing and have their own reactions (my consequences) to them. Thus another element of the Red Thread is that pretense of not knowing what I know.

Self-awareness is based on being fully cognizant of all of these parts, but it also demands being fully present: present to what is happening, present to my roots and experiences that shaped me, present to my thoughts and my emotions, present to the effects and consequences of my actions, and present to the web of inclusion that ties us and all of this together. Learning to honestly answer the "what am I pretending not to know" challenge opens up the discovery of these connective tissues of my being. I can no longer hide in "I don't know" (something I screamed in frustration when Sarah and I were first trying to uncover what might have led to my actions). In being fully aware and fully present, I can see the connective thread linking all of these conditions a condition of blind, unthinking actions.

But learning to become fully present is not an easy task. Many monks spend their lifetime in the pursuit of becoming fully present. And I am of the opinion that while we can learn how to get present, it is extremely difficult to stay in the state of presence for any length of time. So let's take a quick look at how one develops presence. In the next chapter we will look at one model that describes presence as the nexus of letting go of our knowing (or perhaps our presuppositions) and letting the present moment come into us and into our conscience awareness in that moment.

> **Questions to ponder:**
>
> 1. Is there a "red thread" in your life story? What is the common theme that seems to draw it all together?
>
> 2. What are you pretending not to know?
>
> 3. If you asked a half dozen friends to describe your self-awareness, what do you suspect you would hear?

17

A model for presence

For me the model that best captures the nature of the letting go and opening up present is the work of organizational consultant and MIT faculty member, Otto Scharmer. Scharmer describes this undoing process in what he calls his "U" theory. Basing his work on Kurt Lewin's field theory, Scharmer contends that individual behavior is determined by the totality of the individual's context and that organizations (collections of individuals in a specific context) behave just like individuals. Though *Theory U* is primarily an organizational study and applied in the context of economics, its principles describe an individual's surrendering in some ways reminiscent of the AA twelve steps.

Scharmer finds that external pressures force individuals to move from a centralized identity (focused on personal power or a specific skill) to decentralized identity (organized around those defining relationships close to us) to networked awareness (organized around the relationships with those holding key power), and ultimately to what he calls "ecosystems of innovations" (organized around the emerging possibilities discovered only in a co-creative process with everyone involved).[62]

The first few transitions are placed on the left half of the U as the downward movement (shown below). Scharmer labeled the transition at the base of the U, "letting go—letting come," as the transition point that engages a shift toward upward movement to the new state of co-creation. Without first releasing the previously held beliefs in how things

---

62. Otto Scharmer, *Theory U: Leading from the Future as It Emerges* (Cambridge, MA: Society for Organizational Learning, 2007), 303 ff.

must be and must work (or individually—how one defines oneself and who that is), the individual is doomed to repeat the existing pattern and fail to adapt. Previously held beliefs form blinders to being able to see and recognize emerging trends, the natural chaos and turbulence, and the call of disruptive innovation. It is only when the individual (or, for Scharmer, the organization) is open and aware enough to be in co-creation with their surrounding environment that it can adapt and evolve through enacting and embodying a more holistic process.

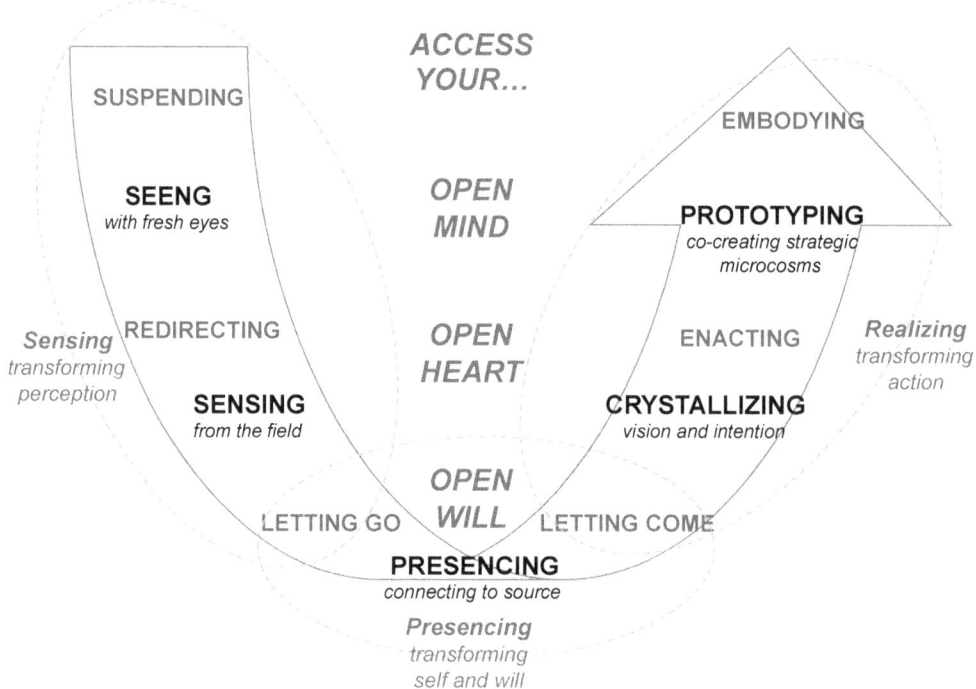

However, Scharmer's model seems to be driven primarily from an internal intention. Though he at times makes reference to external forces (he does claim to be based in Lewin's field system), his entire text seems to come from a context of willful direction. Though it is labeled as "co-creation," Scharmer's actions of crystallizing and enacting are internally driven actions. But the external field must also be a considered force if this is to be true co-creation. In order to have a fuller understanding of that context, we must take into consideration the outside forces that also act on us.

The invisible powers that catalyze and force change on an individual are immense and seemingly irresistible or undeniable powers, driving deeply into the core of one's being. They are the collective beliefs and attitudes of the culture combined with learned interaction patterns of the individual. Theologian, Walter Wink, wrote a series of books on what he calls "The Powers" (a summary of his first three books can be found in his fourth book *The Powers That Be*[63]). In them Wink looks deeply into the role of external forces played throughout biblical and spiritual literature and addresses the "Powers and Principalities" on an internal and external level. Despite the theological nature of his presentation, the principle that we are continually shaped by and reacting to the forces (physical and political) around us applies equally well in our daily functioning. He shows repeatedly how these external forces are the source and catalyst of transformation.

Now, let's drop this down to the practical level of what we are discussing in this book, becoming more present to our emotions and changing (or letting go of) the inner dialogue and assumptions that drive them. Down the center of the U model are labels of the layers of our consciousness, which Scharmer says we must open up in order to fully let go. We first must open our minds, then our heart and finally our will. I choose to interpret that "will" as the inner assumptions that are the source of our self-dialogue. To accomplish this, according to the model, opening our mind requires suspending our judgments about what we "think" we are seeing. Like Descartes, we must become suspicious of any interpretation so that we can begin to see only what is occurring.

Opening our heart requires our looking with compassion on the events and forces surrounding us and the events that are happening. At this point, we experience a kind of foreground/background shift in our perceptions. What was driving our perceptions was our willful interpretive mind but that now takes a back seat as we begin to really perceive what is happening (without judgment). Once we get to that level of perceiving, we become open to seeing what is coming toward us (in spacetime) as the next future and the one after that. This stage Scharmer calls letting go and letting come. We have become open to what is unfolding before us and are better able to respond effectively to that (instead of continually repeating the pattern that our willful judgments produced). Now we become co-creators with the future and crystallize our next actions.

From an emotional perspective, we can see that our foundation for feeling has heretofore been based in previous assessments and beliefs. But when we let go of them, our ability to feel into the next scenario becomes more attuned to what is really present. Scharmer and his colleagues call this "presencing."[64] In other words, our aim in feeling our emotions is one of presencing our true feeling or emotive response so as to be guided in the appropriate direction, free from the beliefs and previously held self-concepts that might otherwise distort our understanding.

Deciding to step on the path is only the first step of engaging in transformation. Once on the path of transformation, the process begins its work on us, pushing us, shaping us and molding us into what we need to become. Wink feels that such is the actual effect of

---

63. Walter Wink, *The Powers that Be* (New York: Random House, 1998).

64. Peter Senge, Otto Scharmer, Joseph Jaworski and Betty Sue Flowers, *Presence: Human Purpose and the Field of the Future* (New York: Currency Doubleday, 2008).

the Powers. While much of Wink's exploration is on identifying and naming the Powers, the significant thing to note is that it is actually the *action* of the Powers that catalyzes the *reaction* of transformation. As Wink notes, despite their seemingly negative nature, "the Powers are good" in that they work toward forcing development and growth. Wink suggests that we might be well served to seek out and engage with these Powers, in that such encounters may be the only path to transformation.

Little more exists in literature that actually describes the transformational journey, and even fewer actual tools and techniques are discussed in direct terms. I might say that one exception is my recently co-authored book, *Typhoon Honey: The Only Way Out Is Through*[65] or my previous book, *Wrestling the Angel: The Role of the Dark Night of the Soul in Spiritual Transformation.*[66] [67]Predominantly, the field of psychology shies away from spiritual matters and relegates most of what might be relevant to the dark night to the realm of depression and psychopathology! Certainly there are references to the use of spiritual discernment (prayerful meditation and listening), and several authors (Benefiel, Ackerman, Rohr to name a few) cite the use of spiritual directors, mentors and coaches for guidance through the disorienting and dissolving aspects of the dark night. But beyond these, there is not much to assist us in actually engaging with that process. What individuals must face during a transition and what they must do to rise to the occasion in a way that positively influences their further evolution and, if successful, their transformation are largely uncharted waters. It is clear that navigating these waters cannot be accomplished by rote process. Each person must blaze his or her own trail—there is no one right way. But it must equally be true that this is *not* the first time such questions have been asked.

Questions to ponder:

1. What new moment, new event, or new you is emerging and wanting to be discovered by you right now?

2. What parts of your mind and will do you get to let go of in order to be more receptive to the oncoming future?

3. What "larger than life" powers are most affecting you or are limiting you in your progress?

---

65. Kris Girrell and Candace Sjogren, *Typhoon Honey: The Only Way Out Is Through* (Hollister, CA: MSI Press, 2021).

66. Kris Girrell, *Wrestling the Angel: The Role of the Dark Night of the Soul in Spiritual Transformation.*(Andover, MA: Kindle Direct Publication, 2015).

67. Additionally, I would recommend Chris Lee's book, *Transform Your Life: Ten Principles of Prosperity and Abundance* (self-published) 2016, and Michael Strasner's *Living on the Skinny Branches: Five Tools to Creating Power, Freedom and a Life Worth Living.* (self-published) 2015.

18

Meditation and Presence

One of the time-tested and most validated methods for building an awareness of presence is the use of meditation. And let me say from the outset that I am no expert in the practice of meditation nor on the myriad methods of practicing meditation. These are just a few of the things I do to move toward being present through meditation.

There are three major different approaches to meditation that I have tried (though I am certain that there are many more). One focuses the mind by using a mantra, chanting, or a sound. A version of this mental focusing style of meditation that I like is to use a sound like a singing bowl, focusing on the sound until it eventually is inaudible and your mind is still.

The second form of meditation is what is referred to as centering prayer or mindfulness meditation. Here we focus on the breath as it flows in and out. One of my meditation teachers said to visualize your breath flowing like the swinging of one of those bar room doors in the old west movies—it just flows back and forth, opening in and opening out. Personally I like to use the sound of my breath as the two syllables of the unspoken name of the Divine (Yahweh): "yah" as the inhalation and "weh" on exhaling. This is done without moving one's lips so as not to speak the name—just breathe it in and out.

And a third method of meditation I have had some success with is walking meditation or movement meditation. Walking a labyrinth is a great example of walking meditation. This entails stilling your mind in the quiet focus of just following the path while simply focusing on placing your feet softly and mindfully on the path. However, movement meditation can be used with any activity—washing the dishes, sweeping the floor, running (especially longer distances), or just a stroll around the neighborhood. For a short period of my life I decided to become a marathon runner. It was a decision I made one day and was not based on my athleticism of the time. In fact I was pretty overweight and out of shape at the time.

I was working in sales at a consulting firm located in the Prudential Center in Boston. This one particular day was the running of the 100th Boston Marathon, and I had a sales call that afternoon around three. We had been watching the elite runners finish from our 20th floor windows, but when I went outside that day, the runners coming past were just regular people trying to do this insane thing of running the distance from Hopkinton, Massachusetts to Boston. As I stood there in the afternoon sun watching people round the corner from Hereford Street onto Boylston, some 460 meters from the finish line, one guy caught my attention. Here was this regular man—not an elite runner—but someone now in his fourth hour since beginning the trek to Boston who, when he saw the finish line down Boylston, did a cartwheel. A cartwheel—out of pure joy in seeing the finish line! He had just run 26 miles and was surely spent, but he did a cartwheel! My immediate reaction was that I wanted to know that feeling. And the only way to know it was to run from Hopkinton all the way to Boston. So right then, without any evidence that I could do it, I declared that I would run a marathon. Not just any marathon—*the* Boston Marathon. After my sales call, I went to the gym and found that I couldn't even run a half mile on the treadmill without stopping. But I was determined to run a marathon—I needed to know what that feeling was.

Boston is a "qualifiers-only" race. You had to have qualified for it by running under three hours in another marathon. I knew that would never happen, so the only option for me was to become a charity runner. The Boston Athletic Association allows a certain number of charity runners from each of several charities to participate in the marathon. The best of these was DFMC, the Dana-Farber Marathon Challenge. So I hounded them with my promise of being able to raise the money until they let me in. I began training with DFMC two weeks later. And they were great. One mile turned to six and then to twelve and fourteen. The pounds fell off my body and I became a runner, and the very next year I entered and completed my first of four Boston Marathons.

But what happened in that process is that I found a meditative state in running. No one wants to go running with you for two hours just for the fun of it! Oh, maybe a buddy will run for four or five miles—but ten or fifteen? No way. So, much of my training time was by myself on these long runs through the state forest and countryside around where I live. Somewhere about six or eight miles out, I would have thought all the thoughts my mind had to offer and it fell silent. Out there, I was just a body—an animal—breathing and running, feeling my pulse and the movement of my limbs. And I became totally thoughtless—I called it headless.[68] It is a meditative state I had never before experienced, and I was at peace and present—extremely present in the moment. That is what movement meditation is to me.

I am certain that there are many other techniques and I'm equally certain that instructors of the art of meditation would debate me on the titles I use, but the bottom line is use whatever works for you. These are the ones I most frequently use.

The main purpose of meditation in my experience was to be able to remove the thoughts about what I am experiencing, much like Scharmer's Opening Mind and Letting Go elements, and to center solely on the experience itself. As I delved more and more into these meditative practices, the awareness that came to me was that emotions held—within them—a type of message or information that I need to understand and act on. Emotions were not inconveniences to be gotten over. They were real and important in some way to our full functioning as a human. And it was that realization that motivated me (much more than the project I was on) to create the *Periodic Table of Human Emotions*.

Learning to meditate is what I would call a sloppy process. It's sloppy in that it is not an exact science. Don't try to get it right—there is no real right way to do it. What you will need to do to begin meditating is to find a quiet space where you won't be interrupted by others or by too many outside noises. Once there, find a comfortable place to sit. I would not suggest that your sitting place be too comfortable as it may put some unnecessary strain on your back. Nor would I suggest that you lie down to try meditation as you may easily fall asleep. That said, there may be nothing wrong about falling asleep either. (See what I mean by sloppy and not exact?)

Soften your gaze or close your eyes, again to minimize your distraction. At this point most teachers suggest you start with a mantra or focusing word or sound. Many find the word OM, which is said to be the Sanskrit representation of the original sound of creation, chanted over and over. And an expansion of that chant is the full Sanskrit verse, "Om Mani Padme Hum" (roughly translated as "The jewel is in the lotus"). Also, as I suggested before, the breathing sound of "Yahweh." Whatever you choose, begin repeating the sound over and over.

Zen teacher and author Pema Chodrun says of meditation that it is like dinnertime at a family house that has two teenagers, a couple of little ones, and some guests. It is crazy and noisy and there are things happening all the time. There are people coming and going and the kids don't often sit still for half of their dinner. But, she says, every once in a while, something happens that you would not want to miss for the world. Meditation and stilling

---

68. The actual concept comes from Douglas Harding who described how he became conscious of his body only while hiking above the tree line in the Himalayas. Harding drew many pictures of himself as what he saw of his body looking down at it (obviously without drawing the head). See Harding's book, *On Having No Head: Zen and the Rediscovery of the Obvious* (London: The Shollond Trust, 2012).

the mind is like that noisy dinner table, but every once in a while, the cacophony stops just enough for some insight or some total peace you get to experience, and you wouldn't want to miss that moment for anything.

> **Questions to ponder:**
>
> 1. What forms of meditation have you tried?
>
> 2. How and when are you most centered in your body and experiences?

19

Becoming Emotionally Intelligent

We finally arrive back at the beginning of this journey, that of learning and practicing Emotional Intelligence. But it is different now. I really believe that the essence of emotional intelligence is rooted in self-awareness and self-understanding. How is it even possible to relate to another's emotional states if one first has no handle on the experience of one's own emotional states and their impact? Throughout this book I have been piecing together what had affected my ability to fully experience my emotions, why and how they got suppressed and buried, what was behind my inability to access my emotion-based motives and needs, and how I might again open up to the experience of the experience called feeling.

That to me is the difficult part of EI. Too often we "think we feel" rather than actually feeling our emotions. And then, even when we have an emotion, far too often it has been tainted by our inner thoughts and self-concepts in such a way that we are more reacting to the inner voices and not to the situation at hand. The intelligence in EI is the ability to become more cognizant of our inner backdrop of self-concepts. It takes hard work and tons of introspection to untangle the mess of what has been handed to us, what we have interpreted from our various experiences, versus the actual "reality" of what has been and is currently going on around us.

For me that took many trips to the well and it required that I continually ask better and better questions of myself. Starting with "what am I pretending not to know?" and digging into what the meaning was that I had placed on my experiences and my education (formal and mostly informal). Coming clean about all of that is not always easy, because it places me squarely in the ownership of all that is going on inside and out.

This is not an exact science, as I have said. There is no rubric or protocol to inform how we name our emotions or how we understand what we are to do as a result of them. Each of us experiences our events and emotions uniquely based in our history, socioeconomic status, education, and past interpretations. Learning emotion words and their distribution across some gradient of experience is helpful for our own understanding. It would not only be wrong but insulting to tell another person who used the emotion word "love" or "disgust" that you thought they were only experiencing "liking" or "being opinionated." Again that would be forcing their experience through our own perceptual lens and would not be the result of any form of emotional intelligence!

So the bottom line of this discussion on understanding emotional experience rests in self-awareness. Learning to feel is all about gaining the clarity on your own experiences and emotions so that we can recognize what is ours and not project that on to another's experience. If and when we gain that clarity and awareness, not only will we be better equipped to listen to the other person's emotional experience, we will be able to identify our internal reaction to what they are describing and use that as a tuning fork. Are we understanding it accurately? What is coming up within our own experience of *their* experience? Would it be helpful to bring that into the conversation?

My good friend, Andy Chaleff, says, "I often tell people, 'I am not really listening to you." (Bullshit; Andy is a great listener.) "Rather," he continues, "I'm listening to how I feel as I hear you. I feel into what is coming up in me as you speak, and what that is telling me about myself and my ideas of you and what you're sharing. This is what guides my questions. The skill is learning to ask meaningful questions. The art is listening to how to hear the voices in your head and connect them to those questions."

But Andy has spent years of training to be able to apply that skill. My experience of him is that he is one of the most self-aware individuals I have ever met. As such, his questions during our conversations are not simply insight-producing, they are scarily accurate and on target. As he says, "Listening does not grant the other side legitimacy. It grants them humanity—and preserves our own."

In other words, when we listen to the other person's experience, irrespective of their ability to describe it with emotional words and labels, we affirm their humanity and their worthiness. Emotional Intelligence, more than anything else, is a process of becoming real and human with each other, without pretense, without guilt or shame, and without the need to force their experience into our personal sense-making system. It frees us both to experience our experiences just as they occur to each of us without labels or interpretation.

There is plenty of time and space for interpretation after you have both created the space for experiencing your respective experiences and after we have each listened and heard what is really going on. Part of why I love my conversations with Andy so much is that there are these long, richly filled periods of silence wherein he is just letting what he heard roll over and over in some sort of savoring process. Occasionally, he'll say "Mmmm" as he further digests what I said before he asks a next question or adds an experience of his own. There is always space in our conversations, yet it is clearly not empty space.

What I have learned from Andy about emotional intelligence is that when I am aware of my internal processes and my self-talk and I am able to clean house of much of my BS, then I can not only hear what another person is saying, I can trust my reactions and experience of them without projecting anything on them.

In the past I understood the four elements of EI: self-awareness, self-management, other-awareness, and the management of others (social management). At that point I was intent on being able to recognize what I thought the other person was experiencing so that I could support or help them out with their situation. But I no longer hold that to be the case.

I do not believe that we can ever know what that other person is actually feeling unless we both ask them and then (and this is imperative) *believe* that what they are reporting to us is their actual experience at that moment. I have no right to judge their level of self-awareness or whether the emotion which they are reporting to me is fraught with negative self-interpretations or coming from tainted past experiences. Emotional intelligence starts with the ability to ask and listen into what the other is telling you. Then, as Andy does, we can sample our own experience of what is being reported and be honest with ourselves and our friend as to our experience of that.

And through this opening up experience of digging into my past and freeing up my emotional experiences, I was finally able to answer that challenge from Sarah:

> "Um, Sarah, can we sit and talk? As I have been writing this book, I think I have cracked the code and have figured some things out about what was going on." We were driving to the Cape, and sometimes driving together is the only dedicated alone time we get.
>
> "Okay—tell me what you learned."
>
> "Well, imagine a big Venn diagram. There's the piece where in not dealing with my dad's death, I started suppressing emotions and pretending that I didn't feel what was going on. That got welded in place when my first wife left."
>
> "Go on."

"Then there's the cultural bit of growing up in Appalachia. I learned that I wasn't worth much without my physical body and that I could have some worth because I was big and strong but also that I had worth through sexuality."

"Wait, I don't get the connection."

"Neither did I until I started weaving this together. I actually had to look up research on poverty and promiscuity to see if it was just me or it was something others did. Turns out that rural poor folks and inner-city poor have a much higher level of promiscuity and teen pregnancies. Additionally, they don't have a sense of future of any kind. So acts are done in the moment in order to feel worth without regard to consequences. That was a killer to learn!"

"I never experienced that growing up, but I don't think we were close enough to subsistence, and I think I had a hell of a lot more self-esteem."

"Yeah. I think that was and still is something I had to deal with. I still struggle with feelings of not enough."

"You bet! I just saw it the other day."

"You mean, when I thought the director wouldn't like me if I could not do the physical part of the job (I had been helping out in Sarah's school with the Toddlers room and it was taking a toll on my back)."

"Exactly. Go on."

"Well another circle is having learned all about various emotions in a detached, academic way instead of through the experience itself."

"Yeah, I have always been very clear about my emotions and what I am feeling."

"I see that in you. Anyway, I had this big piece of pretending not to know—not to know what I was feeling, not to know the future and immediate ramifications of my actions, and not to know what other choices I had. I think writing this has taken away that belief that I don't know."

"Or that you can't remember. You always say, 'I don't think backwards in time.' You claim to be a futurist and think that absolves you from remembering."

"I hear you on that. But writing this opened that all up and I am remembering more of what happened, and of how I was feeling—even if at the time I wasn't fully conscious of that."

"So how do all of those fit together?"

"Well, not wanting to feel the negativity and having hammered flat my emotional ability as a result of my dad's death and my first divorce, I had a convenient mechanism for forgetting. Additionally, a lot of my history has been lined with guilt and shame. But if you don't remember past events you don't have to deal with the shame. Top that all off with never having gotten to a place of feeling that I was enough and you have the perfect storm. But I no longer feel like I am not enough. I am enough and no longer need that outside validation or need to be wanted by someone else anymore."

(After a short period of silence) "I have a question: Remember when the business failed and you left one night—to go stay with your daughter? What were you feeling then?" (Is that a test or are you just being good conversationalist, Sarah?)

"I felt so alone, like no one understood how much I was hurting. And you said something about it just being a business. That hurt. Because it was so much more than that. And because I was such a raw nerve, I just had to get away to some safe refuge, and I thought Becca might be able to provide that."

I remembered!

I recalled the full barrage of emotions and could still feel some residual emotionality in the moment as I described the event. I was feeling it and all I had felt then. Test or no test, whatever this process has been, it has unblocked my emotional dam. Those emotions were all there—and they had been there all along, despite not being able to access them at any given time.

Emotional Intelligence relies heavily on empathy and empathy starts with self-awareness—not just the cognitive elements of knowing who you are but with the fullness of the emotional being that you are. Being self-aware means that you know what your feelings are, what the events and interpretations are that are at the source of those emotions, and, importantly, knowing what is yours and what is someone else's.

That last part is the really hard part for a couple of reasons. First of all, we only really know ourselves in relation to others and other things around us. We actually discover ourselves through those interactions, whether that is with another person or, for example, a heavy object ("I am stronger than that stone I just moved" "I was humbled by the climb up that mountain"). Was it the stone's weight that was revealed or my relative strength or weakness?

Those are simple examples. But when it comes to knowing ourselves through relationships, it becomes so much more complex. At first, when we are younger, the boundaries between self and other are relatively blurred. As we mature, however, we begin to own our own feelings and states. You may have to spend what seems like an inordinate amount of time learning that your feelings are entirely yours and that, therefore, you have agency over them!

Untangling the webs of illusion and interpretations feels cleaner—less messy—somehow. Knowing what my feelings and thoughts are, I can better see or hear what another person is experiencing. None of us will ever "know" what the other person is feeling—fully. We must ask, listen, and believe their report—even when or if we believe that they are not aware of *their* emotions or not aware of what is causing them to act and feel a certain way. Only when we give them agency and credibility are we able to engage with them in any kind of emotionally intelligent way.

But when we do, we can perhaps get to the place from which Andy Chaleff operates. We can then listen to our reaction to the other person as a reverberation or sounding board and share our experience and feelings with our friend in a way that advances the conversation and perhaps their processing of what is going on. Operating on the supposition that we actually know what is going on for them is not only a fallacy, it can be a detriment to the relationship, come across as patronizing and even close off further exploration.

> "When you just said that, I got a shiver in my body," Andy told me.
>
> "What do you mean?"
>
> "My experience of you is that you are often quite aware of your surroundings and what is going on inside yourself. But when you just brushed that off as 'not knowing,' it didn't fit with who you are. I am like a tuning fork and I reverberate—even with shivers in my body— when something doesn't fit with my knowing of who you are."
>
> "Hmmm, let me dig deeper into that. I think what I meant was I couldn't access it at the time. But now that you stopped me from just glossing over it, I do recall what I was thinking and feeling at the time."
>
> "Your mind or your ego doesn't like having all those feelings," Andy continued, "and so it has developed this brush off habit over time. You just need to recognize that it's a bad habit—but it doesn't mean that you don't know."

Andy didn't tell me I was wrong. Nor did he postulate what he thought might be going on for me. He simply reported on what his experience of me was and it led me to open up more. It furthered the conversation.

Emotional intelligence is growing up, a maturing or ripening of sorts that helps me and my mind to be fully present to the internal dialogues, emotions, and reactions as well as to the surroundings or contexts in which that is happening. I have experienced a profound shift that moves from looking for confirmation and validation externally to the place where I have begun to trust the wisdom I have learned on the back side of those hurts, pains, failures, and misinterpretations. When we do that, we no longer see ourselves as the center of the universe but just a tiny sliver—one seven billionth—of the human experience. And with that awareness of immensity, contrasted with the awareness of our own individual experience in the context of our finite smallness, we emerge with a deepening understanding and respect for "others."

In maturity we open up to the awareness of the way things are and such that we can actually find a level of acceptance. But don't read acceptance as rolling over to play dead! Acceptance is a clear-eyed look into the reality of life. It is becoming fully present to what actually is. In previous chapters I talked at length about how we never see things as they are—that we only see through our perceptual filters. But in the maturation process we are finally letting go of those old filters because we are learning that we (and our long-held beliefs) don't matter near as much as our striving to understand what is outside of us for its own value.

We no longer hold on to those unessential and often unreal beliefs. We recognize that it feels almost childish to hold on to them and find that they have begun just falling away. It is not so much that we have so totally evolved that we actually see reality completely free from our interpretation. Rather, it is that we know the difference and can see the difference between what is "out there" and what we believe it must be.

Nowhere is this clearer than in the realm of relationships, listening, and particularly emotional intelligence. I think that is what Andy points us to—that is, listening to another without an opinion, and without our filters so that we can, first of all, actually hear what is said and meant by the other, and secondly so that we can freely feel into that experience as a barometer of the relationship. Our feelings allow us to experience the space between us and our friends and loved ones instead of the almost self-centered reactivity with which we are so accustomed.

So let's unpack the fullness of emotional intelligence, version 4.0! We will still stick with the four-box layout, but now we look at it from a different perspective. We will retain the self-awareness and other-awareness, but now we look at those two from an understanding of life that sees both the experience and emotions as well as the stories and interpretations we have been so righteously holding on to.

But the other dimension becomes more about the response effectiveness and not the management of those feeling states. We need not manage them if we understand their origins and interpretations. Responding is not reacting. Reactions come from our embedded, unchallenged beliefs and experiences. Responding, on the other hand, is a choice point based in a clearer understanding of what is going on inside of self and other.

I had always experienced the language of Solvay & Meyer and Goleman's emotional intelligence descriptions as a tad manipulative. It seemed as the purpose was to be able to "manage" people better, and, of course, that is to some extent true. In addition, managing one's own feelings and emotions landed on me like "getting over" them —just deal with it!

But what I have come to as an understanding of emotional intelligence has radically shifted from that more fix-it mentality to one of clean understanding and responsiveness. I must learn the depth of meaning-making behind my emotional states in order to understand where they come from and where they might be directing me.

And in understanding my inner workings more fully, I am not only able to have a cleaner (less encumbered by past interpretations) experience of the emotional experience itself, I am able to more effectively choose my response. The same is true when I have a cleaner (less filtered by my own issues, reactions, and emotions) experience of the other person's emotional state. But what has shifted more is that rather than my attempting to intuit what another is feeling, I will ask them what they are feeling. Perhaps, more importantly, I will trust their report unless they say that they don't know how they are feeling at the time, in which case I will patiently ask for them to be a bit more introspective and see what emerges.

The chart on the opposite page describes how I have adapted the Salovey & Mayer and Goleman two by two model of emotional intelligence from a cross between self and others with awareness and management to one of personal and relational with understanding and responsiveness.

Actual emotional intelligence is mature understanding of the human condition for all parties and it requires our continual development and "ripening" into maturity. Fruit that is picked before it has fully ripened is sour or bitter—but certainly not as sweet and nourishing as the ripe version. Even when we don't pick all the ripe fruit, it will fall to the ground and become the food that nourishes the seed to grow a new plant; to regenerate and become the next iteration of the fruit. Ripening is the model the world presents to us and it is never more applicable as a model than in the realm of emotions. But to be clear, it is not the emotions that are ripening. Rather, it is we who are ripening in our awareness and understanding of self and other (or not-self).

How then do we practice this EI thing? What are some practices that will help us not only be emotionally responsive but emotionally responsible as well?

1. First of all listen to your emotions from the perspective of the direction (motion) that they are suggesting. In simple terms thinking of things like love tells us to move toward and fear tells us to move away. Each emotion has a message that can help us understand our situation. This has become my regular routine—checking in on how I feel about things.

	Understanding	Responsiveness
Personal - Self/mind/body/emotion	Learning to differentiate between my experiences and the interpretations of those emotions and experiences. • Aware of self and behavioral reactions • Aware of underlying beliefs • Separates thoughts from the feelings they produce	Responding to the emotions from choice and not from habit. Maturing into the ability to choose our responses free from the knee-jerk reactions of the past • Is adaptable and resilient • Growth mindset • Exercises emotional self-control • Acts with integrity
Relational – Others and context	Knowing that the same distinctions exist for the other person, we ask, and more importantly, we believe what they report to us as authentically theirs. • Asks and is curious about others' thoughts and feelings • Demonstrates understanding, empathy, and compassion	Experiencing our own sensations in listening into the other person's situation. Asking questions that further their understanding of their situation, state, and reactions. • Builds relationships and connections • Focuses on collaborating and cooperation

2. But at the same time, let's not give too much credence to our emotions because we know that they mostly are the products of our thinking. I attempt to challenge each emotional reaction by looking for what thoughts preceded the feeling and to inspect those thoughts for whether they come from old, dysfunctional stories or from a sound analysis.

3. Not all emotions have to be acted on. (Another reminder to myself). Start learning to discern which emotions are "just feelings" and which are messengers. As humans we will always feel—it's how we are built—but some of them just get to be passing states that we do not have to do anything about. Think for example of the joy and serenity you feel while looking at a beautiful sunset or the peace you feel in the arms of your lover. There is nothing to fix there!

4. Ask others what they are feeling and accept that as their truth without judgment ("you shouldn't feel that way"). Furthermore, refrain from trying to make people feel better. I was recently telling someone about how upset I was with our current

state of affairs, and he immediately started trying to lift my spirits until I told him to stop—that I was okay with the experience of the feelings I was having.

5. Discuss your emotions with transparency—especially with your significant others and close friends. Having emotional conversations can fill in the blanks and help your friend or partner better understand all of what you are going through. Try, however, to increase your emotional vocabulary. If you are continually referring to your feelings with just the few labels of happy, sad, mad, and glad, you aren't providing much clarity. This is the bottom line to which Sarah had been leading me!

6. Accept all of your feelings as information without further labeling them as good or bad. Just because an emotion feels bad doesn't mean that it is not good for you. As we have discussed at length, some of the heavier emotions act as catalysts for moving us through our pain or difficulties and can drive us to learn more about how to get better and avoid such crashes and failures in the future. From this perspective, it is now quite clear to me that these are the real power tools of transformation.

7. Use your emotions to develop compassion for yourself. Be gentle with allowing your emotional self to come into being. Be tender with yourself when you are hurting, sad, embarrassed, depressed, and so on. Developing compassion for yourself will allow you to build the capacity for compassion for others. If there was one unexpected by-product of this work, it has been to develop a deep compassion for me, my life, and the experiences that have shaped me.

Armed with these tools and a much deeper awareness of my own feelings, I am now able to listen to what Sarah is asking of me and finally understand that it is not an inspection of my worth. She is and has most always been (at least within our thirty-year marriage) emotionally intelligent. She is listening for what is going on in me and not allowing me to be numbed or blinded to the deeper messages in my experience. I had a recent call with Coach Amy.

> Coach: So how did the conversation go with Sarah?
>
> Me: Well, I told her what was being revealed as I went through the writing process, how taking the time to ask myself what must have happened instead of pretending that I couldn't remember or access that opened me up to remembering.
>
> Coach: That sounds like progress to me, what do you think?
>
> Me: I also discovered how denying that I could remember things, allowed me to not feel the guilt and shame of previous events. I've been experiencing a flood of new memories that have been obscured for quite some time.

Coach: That is huge. So where are you now with all of this?

Me: I think I feel free. No. I *feel* free! I feel like a heaviness has been lifted away from me. I feel lighter— mmm, maybe cleaner. You know, I really want to thank you for helping me find this depth of being.

Coach: YOU did the work, my friend. I just continued to ask questions.

Me: Yeah, well that worked, is working, and I don't want to stop. So, thank you.

Last week, my friend, Stacy, herself an accomplished coach and psychologist, called me to support her in dealing with a process that just didn't feel right. Her "Spidey Senses" were saying that something just didn't add up. In the conversation we got to look at what transpired with her business client, what she was making her emotions mean, and at what was hers and what was the client's. At the conclusion of our call, Stacy thanked me for my time and for being the listening ear she had needed. That's how this journey has helped me, and more importantly, it has helped my relationships and my ability to be present to my friends and loved ones.

The journey of the wounded healer is one of expanding, not shrinking. Everything that we used to think of as a hit or an arrow to the chest opens us up to a greater experience of our humanity and of humanity as a whole. I have learned from my having been coached by my friend Amy, by Stacy, and immensely by Andy. Each has a perspective that I have learned to cherish.

Andy taught me a question that I have started using in these emotional quests. Instead of asking myself what I should *do* next, I have begun asking myself, "What am I most afraid of in this moment?" It opens me up to vulnerability and to experiencing my experience. And usually, leaning into that fear by naming it and answering the subsequent follow-up questions (like what is behind that), I am able to identify the source belief and "park it" so that I am better able to listen to my internal dialogue and to what others are reporting as their experience.

Andy's book, *The Wounded Healer*,[69] ends with this paragraph, and I cannot think of anything that expresses my feelings better. "Yes, I am a wounded healer and pain is my greatest teacher. To the thousands of people who shared in this journey, I say, 'I love you. Truly. Your willingness to join me will never be forgotten.'"

So, in the final analysis, perhaps emotional intelligence is not so much about *intelligence* at all. It is not a thing that one "knows" or some sort of knowledge one amasses over time. Rather I think that emotional intelligence is perhaps a deep awareness of the experiences

---

69. Andy Chaleff, *The Wounded Healer: A Journey in Radical Self-Love.* (Virginia Beach, VA: Koehler Books, 2020).

we have seen through the perspective of our emoting. It is like some window that after cleaning it sufficiently, one can see through more clearly.

I have never been a smoker, and the car I drive has never been driven by a smoker. But strangely, the inside of the windshield keeps getting a smoky haze to it that I must clean time and time again. Our emotional awareness is like that—we may not contribute to the haze, but there it is, clouding our view and in need of another cleaning. And if there is intelligence to be had about emotional awareness, it is knowing that we must continually clean the window through which we view our own emotions and of the emotions of our friends. Perhaps we may never see or hear clearly or completely, totally without our own bias or perspective, but we can become good custodians of the window through which we view our emotions and the emotions of our friends and associates.

Learning to Feel is just the start of your enriched life experience. Being able to tap into your emotional powers and being able to listen to others' experience unlocks not only a new level of relatedness with your friends, family, and associates, your deeper awareness empowers you to use that internal guidance system to be able to feel confident that your perceptions are no longer "reactions" to the world. They are conscious choices that allow you to become a force for change toward a greater level of humanity and interconnectedness with those you love. With an arsenal of clear emotions you can create a deeper bond than you have ever experienced before. Seeing clearly into the full spectrum of the human experience is a gift for which you will be forever grateful—one for which I would not exchange for any amount of money in the world.

May you have the same blessings on your path to wholeness.

Questions to Ponder:

1. Draw out a life line of your own, placing the major events and experiences that have shaped you. What events are harder to remember?

2. Which have taught you what you are and what you aren't capable of? What have your wounds taught you?

3. How might you establish a practice of listening to the inner dialogue as a reflection of your experience of the other person in the conversation?

20

Epilogue to the Second Edition

How It Plays Out

As this book was originally going to press, I had to undergo some rather invasive and painful surgery. The years of abuse through athletics had taken a toll on my lumbar spine. Not only had the stenosis almost totally constricted my spinal cord in multiple locations, it had also caused scarring all along the dura (the membranous sheath of the cord). Surgeons had to open the vertebrae and then scrape the scarring off before reinserting the cord and patching the whole thing up, including a couple of bars and screws for support.

To say that the post-operative pain was intense is a major understatement! While Sarah stayed with me during the surgery and recovery, she had to be at the office the next few days and could only visit for a few hours on Friday and Sunday. What happened afterwards is, in my thinking, a miracle and a direct result of having done the work of writing this book.

Sunday evening Sarah called, feeling stressed by the pressures of her job and all the household chores I normally do. I was only to have been in the hospital for a day or two, but due to the severity of the procedure, I was going to have to stay a full week. That put all the pressure of doing the work of two people squarely on her.

Here's the miracle. My normal knee-jerk reaction would have been, "Hey, what about me? I'm the one in pain and hospitalized," but the immediate series of thoughts that followed in the next few seconds took me back to where I had first felt like that. I was six years old and playing on some monkey bars next door when I fell from the top, about ten or twelve feet, to the concrete pad below. Because I instinctively broke my fall with my arm, it had broken in three places (although all I knew as a kid of six was that it hurt like hell).

I went home crying and as it was just past noon. My mom said I should lie down and rest and that Dad would know what to do. The pain kept getting worse. By the time my father got home from work, the arm had begun to swell, but he thought it was just a bad bruise and that we should put ice on it and put me to bed. I remember crying most of the night, thinking that no one believed me that it hurt so much. The next morning it looked bad enough that I was taken to the hospital for x-rays. The kicker was that since I was six and my growth hormones were in full swing, the three fractures had started knitting and would have to be re-broken. I remember the medical team weighing down my arm with sandbags for the x-rays before they put me under to set the bones again. It seemed that no one listened to me when I kept saying that it hurt.

The net of this entire memory a moment later was the feeling of not being heard about my pain. But just as quickly as that had occurred, I remembered that when Sarah was just a teen, her father was suddenly paralyzed and her mother, who had been the pampered one in her family, had no way to cope with it, let alone understanding how to take care of five kids of her own. The result was that Sarah took over the parenting duties and went from teen to adult overnight. I was suddenly overcome with a deep compassion for her, and the resulting conversation opened up a wonderfully sweet and loving exchange. No one had heard her just as no one had heard me. Our respective pains allowed us to hear and care about each other.

The work of learning to feel is all about discovering what is behind and undergirding your emotional reactions. Had I not done this work, the result would have been my being snippy at best and perhaps whining and accusatory at worst. That it wasn't showed me that I had learned the source of my feelings, and that knowledge had unlocked this hidden memory I had not even discovered (or recalled) when I was writing the original text. The feelings of "not enough" and "nobody hears or cares about my truth" were not only the source for what happened that Sunday night, but also they lay buried in memory and probably had been setting off so many other times when those feelings resulted in my acting less mature (perhaps more like a six-year-old) and often caused more damage.

It is my sincere hope that in reading this and reflecting on the questions after each chapter, you too may begin to uncover lost and forgotten elements of your development that are still at work producing less-than-effective (emotionally driven) responses to your daily grown-up life. Learning to feel lifts us out of our past, pre-programmed reactions into the present tense ability to respond to ourselves, our current situations, and our present day loved ones. May this work for you as well.

Many blessings,
Kris Girrell

Works Cited

Alexander, Cheryl S., Margaret E. Ensminger, Young J. Kim, B. Jill Smith, Karin E. Johnson, and Lawrence J. Dolan. "Early Sexual Activity among Adolescents in Small Towns and Rural Areas: Race and Gender Patterns." *Family Planning Perspectives* 21, No. 6 (Nov. - Dec., 1989): 261-266.

Barrett, Lisa Feldman. *How Emotions are Made: The Secret Life of the Brain.* New York: Houghton Mifflin, 2017.

Bartsch, Karl, Elizabeth Yost, and Kris Girrell. *Effective Personal and Career Decision Making.* Washington, DC: Westinghouse Learning Corp., 1976.

Benefiel, Margaret. *The Soul of a Leader: Finding Your Path to Success and Fulfillment.* New York: Crossroad Publishing, 2008.

Bly, Robert. *Selected Poems of Rainer Maria Rilke*, edited and translated by Robert Bly. New York: Harper & Row, 1981.

Bostick, Mike. Emotion Wheel. 2018. Accessed at https://observablehq.com/@mbostock/emotion-wheel.

Brown, Brené. *Atlas of the Heart: Mapping Meaningful Connection and the Language of Human Experience.* New York: Penguin Random House, 2021.

"Brené Brown explains the misconceptions around guilt and shame." ABC News Australia. Dec. 1, 2021. https://www.abc.net.au/news/2021-12-02/brene-brown-ted-talk-emotions-shame-guilt-misconceptions-covid19/100669362?utm_campaign=abc_news_web&utm_content=link&utm_medium=content_shared&utm_source=abc_news_web

Daring Greatly: How the Courage to Be Vulnerable Transforms the Way We Live, Love, Parent, and Lead. New York: Penguin Random House, 2012.

"Listening to shame."2012. TED Video: 20:22. https://www.ted.com/talks/brene_brown_listening_to_shame?language=en

Chaleff, Andy. *The Connection Playbook: How to Create Deep Harmony Within Yourself and Others.* Virginia Beach, VA: Koehler Books, forthcoming, 2022).

The Wounded Healer: A Journey in Radical Self-Love. Virginia Beach, VA: Koehler Books, 2020.

Chierotti, Logan. "Harvard Professor Says 95% of Purchasing Decisions Are Subconscious." *Inc. Magazine*, March 26, 2018.

Descartes, René. "Meditations on First Philosophy." *Internet Encyclopedia of Philosophy*, 1996.

Damasio, Antonio. *Descartes' Error.* New York: Penguin/Vintage Books, 1994. Reprinted, Vintage Books, 2006.

Darwin, Charles. *The Expression of The Emotions in Man and Animals.* 4th ed. London: Oxford University Press, Anniversary edition, 2009.

Drummond, Tom. Vocabulary of Emotions/Feelings. https://tomdrummond.com/wp-content/uploads/2019/11/Emotion-Feelings.pdf

Erikson, Erik. *Identity, Youth and Crisis.* New York: W.W. Norton & Co., 1994.

Fiene, Judith Ivy. "The Social Reality of a Group of Rural, Low-Status Appalachian Women: A Grounded Theory Study. " PhD diss., University of Tennessee, 1988. https://trace.tennessee.edu/utk_graddiss/4033.

Fisher, Roger, and William Ury. *Getting to Yes: Negotiating Agreement without Giving In.* New York: Penguin Books, 1981.

FitzGerald, Constance. "Impasse and Dark Night." In *Living with Apocalypse, Spiritual Resources for Social Compassion.* Edited by Tilden Edwards, 93-116. San Francisco: HarperCollins, 1984.

Fowler, James. *Stages of Faith: The Psychology of Human Development and the Quest for Meaning.* New York: HarperOne, 1981.

Freire, Paulo. *Pedagogy of the Oppressed, 50th Anniversary Edition.* New York: Bloomsbury Academic, 2018.

Gilbert, Dan. *Stumbling on Happiness*. New York: Vintage/Random House, 2005.

Gilligan, Carol. *The Birth of Pleasure: A New Map of Love*. New York: Vintage/Random House, 2002.

In a Different Voice: Psychological Theory and Women's Development. Cambridge, MA: Harvard University Press, 2009.

Girrell, Kris. *Wrestling the Angel: The Role of the Dark Night of the Soul in Spiritual Transformation*. Andover, MA: Kindle Direct Publishing, 2015.

Girrell, Kris, and Candace Sjogren. *Typhoon Honey: The Only Way Out is Through*. Hollister, CA: MSI Press, 2021.

Harding, Douglas. *On Having No Head: Zen and the Rediscovery of the Obvious*. London: The Shollond Trust, 2012.

Kahneman, Daniel, and Amos Tversky. "Prospect Theory: An Analysis of Decision Under Risk." *Econometrica*, 47, no. 2, (March 1979).

Keen, Sam. *To Love and Be Loved*. New York: Bantam Books, 1999.

Kumar Das, Shyamal, Asharf Esmail, and Lisa Eargle. "Men's Exploration of Multiple Sexual Partners: Economic vs Psychosocial Explanation." *Bangladesh e-Journal of Sociology*. 2009, 6, no. 1.

Loder, James. *The Logic of the Spirit: Human Development in Theological Perspective*. San Francisco: Jossey-Bass, 1998.

Milhausen, Robin R., Richard Crosby, William L Yarber, Ralph J DiClemente, Gina M Wingood, Kele Ding. "Rural and nonrural African American high school students and STD/HIV sexual-risk behaviors**.**" *American Journal Health Behavior* 27, no. 4 (July-August 2003): 373-9, https://pubmed.ncbi.nlm.nih.gov/12882431/.

Plutchik, Robert. "A General Psychoevolutionary Theory of Emotion." In *Theories of Emotion*, edited by R. Plutchik and H. Kellerman, 3-33. Vol. 1. New York: Academic Press, 1980.

Real, Terrence. *I Don't Want to Talk About It*. New York: Scribner, 1997.

Salovey, P., and J.D. Mayer. "Emotional Intelligence." *Imagination, Cognition, and Personality* 9, no. 3 (1989-1990): 185–211.

Scharmer, Otto. *Theory U: Leading from the Future as It Emerges*. Cambridge, MA: Society for Organizational Learning, 2007.

Schwartz, Barry. *The Paradox of Choice: Why More Is Less*. New York: Harper Perennial, 2004.

Scott, Susan, *Fierce Conversations: Achieving Success In Work and Life One Conversation at a Time*. New York: Penguin Group, 2002.

Senge, Peter, Otto Scharmer, Joseph Jaworski, and Betty Sue Flowers. *Presence: Human Purpose and the Field of the Future*. New York: Currency Doubleday, 2008.

St. John of the Cross. *Dark Night of the Soul*. Translated by Mirabai Starr. New York: Riverhead, 2002.

Tillich, Paul, *Love, Power and Justice: Ontological Analysis and Ethical Applications*. London: Oxford University Press, 1960.

Weil, Simone. *Waiting for God*. Translated by Emma Craufurd. New York: G. P. Putnam's Sons, 1951, 112.

Wiesel, Elie. *Night*. New York: Hill and Wang, 1958.

Wilcox, Gloria. "The Feeling Wheel." *Transactional Analysis Journal* 12, No. 4 (1982): 274-276.

Wilson, Bill. *Alcoholics Anonymous: The Story of How Thousands of Men and Women Have Recovered from Alcoholism*. 4th ed. New York: AAWS, 2001.

Wink, Walter. *The Powers that Be*. New York: Random House, 1998.

Songs

Beatles. "I Want to Hold your Hand." YouTube. Universal Music Group. Remastered 2015. EMI Studios. Originally released in 1963. https://www.youtube.com/watch?v=g_zg50NMwXc

Billy Joe Royal. "Cherry Hill Park." Legacy Recordings. January 23, 1985. Columbia Records. Originally released in 1969. https://soundcloud.com/billy-joe-royal/cherry-hill-park-1

Bob Dylan. "Lay Lady Lay." Big Sky Music. 1997. Columbia Records. Originally released in 1969. https://www.bobdylan.com/songs/lay-lady-lay/

Bob Seger. *Night Moves*. Capitol Records, 1976.

Hayley Mills. "Let's Get Together." Disney, 1961.

Led Zepplin. "The Lemon Song." Atlantic Records, 1969.

Mungo Jerry. "In the Summertime." UnionSquare Music. 2020. UnionSquare Music. Originally released in 1970. https://mungojerry.lnk.to/InTheSummertimeID

Kinks. "Lola." Davray Music, Ltd. 1970. https://secondhandsongs.com/work/23172

Peter Gabriel. "Digging in the Dirt." Peter Gabriel. 2018. Geffen Records. Originally released in 1992. https://www.youtube.com/watch?v=6JeZ8nbSMSE

Robert Palmer. "Sneakin' Sally Through the Alley." Robert Palmer. 2018. Compass. Originally released in 1974. https://www.youtube.com/watch?v=skqARFhEHxg

Rolling Stones. "Let's Spend the Night Together." Rolling Stones. 2012. RCA Records. Originally released in 1967. https://www.youtube.com/watch?v=9YADLsz367Q

Rolling Stones. "(I Can't Get No) Satisfaction." London Records. Originally released in 1965. https://www.45cat.com/record/459766

Them. "Gloria." Decca Records, 1964 (later released as a very sexually loaded live recording by the Doors in 1971).

OTHER BOOKS BY KRIS GIRRELL

Typhoon Honey (Girrell & Sjogren)

SELECT BOOKS FROM MSI PRESS

57 Steps to Paradise (Lorenz)

A Guide to Bliss (Tubali)

A Movie Lover's Search for Romance (Charnas)

A Woman's Guide to Self-Nurturing (Romer)

Anger Anonymous (Ortman)

Anxiety Anonymous (Ortman)

Depression Anonymous (Ortman)

Divorced! (Romer)

El Poder de lo Transpersonal (Ustman)

How My Cat Made Me a Better Man (Feig)

How to Get Happy and Stay That Way (Romer)

How to Live from Your Heart (Hucknall)

How to Stay Calm in Chaos (Gentile)

Life, Liberty, & COVID-19 (Ortman)

Mental Health Mayday (G Bagdade)

Noah's New Puppy (R. Rice, V. Rice, & Henderson)

Old and On Hold (Cooper)

Rainstorm of Tomorrow (Dong)

Road Map to Power (A. Husain & D. Husain)

Road to Damascus (E. Imady)

Seeking Balance in an Unbalanced Time (Greenebaum)

Staying Safe While Sheltering in Place (Schnuelle, Adams, & Henderson)

Survival of the Caregiver (Snyder)

The Invisible Foreign Language Classroom (Dabbs & Leaver)

The Optimistic Food Addict (Fisanick)

The Pandemic and Hope (Ortman)

The Rose and the Sword (Bach & Hucknall)

The Seven Wisdoms of Life (Tubali)

The Widower's Guide to a New Life (Romer)

Understanding the Analyst (Quinelle)

Understanding the Critic (Quinelle)

Understanding the Entrepreneur (Quinelle)

Understanding the People around You (Filatova)

Understanding the Seeker (Quinelle)

Widow: A Survival Guide for the First Year (Romer)

Widow: How to Survive (and Thrive!) in Your 2nd, 3rd, and 4th Years

www.ingramcontent.com/pod-product-compliance
Lightning Source LLC
Chambersburg PA
CBHW061117170426
43199CB00026B/2949